INFORMATION TECHNOLOGY IN SCHOOLS

The role of the school librarian and the teacher

INFORMATION TECHNOLOGY IN SCHOOLS

The role of the school librarian and the teacher

Second edition of *The microcomputer, the school librarian and the teacher*

James E. Herring
Senior Lecturer, Information Management,
Queen Margaret College, Edinburgh

LIBRARY ASSOCIATION PUBLISHING
LONDON
A Clive Bingley Book

© Library Association Publishing Ltd, 1987, 1992

Published by
Library Association Publishing Ltd
7 Ridgmount Street
London WC1E 7AE

First published 1987 as *The microcomputer, the school librarian and the teacher*
This second edition 1992

British Library Cataloguing in Publication Data

Herring, James E.
  Information Technology in Schools: Role of the
  School Librarian and the Teacher.
  — 2Rev.ed
  I. Title
  027.80285416

  ISBN 1-85604-055 0

Typeset from author's disks in 10/11pt Palacio by Library Association Publishing Ltd
Printed and made in Great Britain by Bookcraft (Bath) Ltd.

Contents

Contributors

Nigel Akers is Coordinator, Key Stage 3 at Djanogly City Technology College, Nottingham.

Julia Allen is Librarian at The Ruskin School, Crewe.

Angela Bell is Librarian, Holywells High School, Ipswich.

Jan Condon is Librarian at Solihull Sixth Form College, Solihull.

James E. Herring is a Senior Lecturer in Information Management, Queen Margaret College, Edinburgh.

Anne Johnston is Librarian at Dunbar Grammar School, Dunbar.

Shirley Matthews is IT Librarian, Hertfordshire Schools Library Service.

Margaret Smith is Senior Adviser, Cambridgeshire Schools Library Service.

Dorothy Williams is Lecturer in the School of Librarianship and Information Studies, The Robert Gordon University, Aberdeen.

Morea Wood is Senior Librarian, Resources, in Cheshire Education Library Service.

Acknowledgements

I would like to thank all the contributors for their excellent chapters but thanks must also go to others who helped:
Chapter 1 – Jan Condon, Elizabeth Lavin and Tom Howard, Richard Cramp, Pam Dalby; Chapter 3 – Mike Trotter; Chapter 6 – Bronwyn Robertson; Chapter 7 – Cameron Muir.

Love and thanks also must go to Val, Jonathan and Stuart for their support.

James E. Herring

Introduction

James E. Herring

Since the first edition of this book five years ago, there have been numerous changes in secondary schools in the UK and elsewhere. Perhaps the most dramatic, in educational terms, has been the introduction of the National Curriculum which has led teachers and school librarians to look afresh at what is taught in schools, how subjects are taught, what resources are required and, perhaps most importantly, how effective learning can be encouraged.

In terms of technology, the last five years have seen a leap in the sophistication of technology in schools. In the UK, many (but by no means all) schools have moved on from reliance on the BBC microcomputer to the use of IBM compatibles, the Apple Macintosh and the Acorn Archimedes. Schools now *expect* microcomputers to have hard disks, more sophisticated software and options for CD-ROM and multimedia. Pupils' expectations of microcomputers are also rising. The increasing use of scanners and laser printers in some schools has ensured that pupils are now conscious of quality in the presentational aspects of their projects and essays. Desktop publishing, which existed in schools five years ago in a fairly unsophisticated way, is now another accepted facility in many schools. There are still, however, many schools where the knowledge of new technology and its applications is not matched by the school's ability to purchase either hardware or software. In this context, little has changed in five years in that a school's financial status is still a determinant factor in the provision of information technology in the school.

In terms of software, the quality and range have greatly increased. For school librarians in particular, the growing availability of a wide range of CD-ROM products, some of which are multimedia, has meant that sources of information which were traditionally expensive (e.g. encyclopedias) and difficult to cross-search are now available. In some cases, for example Hypercard, new methods of storing, presenting and retrieving information have appeared in the past five years. The developments in software are so rapid that it is salutary to remember that hypertext software was not generally available before the mid-1980s. Other software packages, such as word processors, spreadsheets and databases are now much more widely used in schools. The dynamic rate of change can be seen in the fact that many sixth-year pupils, who have lived through this change, can look back on their early secondary school years and point to the *lack* of hardware, software and opportunities to use computers in the library or in the classroom.

One aspect that has not changed in the past five years is that, in educational terms, the use of information by pupils is of far greater importance than their use of technology. Much is heard of the importance of 'computer literacy' – a term usually meant to denote the ability to use efficiently various information technologies. What educationists are concerned with, however, is the *effective* use of information technology, i.e. the effective use of information. Thus the term 'information literacy' would more accurately describe what teachers and school librarians would like to see in their pupils. Information literacy would encompass the pupils' awareness of the need to identify a purpose for information; the pupils' ability to locate appropriate sources of information; and the pupils' ability to use effectively the relevant information found. 'Computer literacy' would tend to suggest mechanical ability whereas 'information literacy' relates to cognitive skills. Thus pupils are expected to be able to employ skills in evaluating ideas and concepts in the information sources they use and not merely to be able to know how to load and operate a range of software.

A number of research projects focusing on the need to link the use of information technology to information skills in schools have shown how information technology can improve the pupils' approach to the use of information. Projects such as 'Learning information technology skills'[1] have examined how new sources of information, e.g. online information databases, while providing pupils with access to a greater amount and range of information, demand that pupils pay even more attention to the need for adequate search strategies which relate to the use pupils will make of the information retrieved.

The first edition of this book stated that the focus of the book was 'on school librarians and teachers working together and using microcomputers for educational ends'.[2] The changes in technology do not alter the focus of the present book. The professional skills of both the school librarian who is knowledgeable about the development of information skills, the creation and use of databases and the acquisition, processing and organization of learning resources, and the teacher who has individual subject knowledge, curriculum planning and implementation skills and an appreciation of the abilities of pupils, when combined, are a powerful force for improving teaching and learning in any school. The benefits to pupils in terms of their acquisition of information handling and processing skills, including their ability to use databases to find and exploit learning resources, are seen in schools where IT has been used to good effect and where improvements in pupils' motivation and in the quality of their work are evident.

This book offers school librarians and teachers a wide variety of aspects of IT use in schools. An overview of developments in the use of IT in schools and in particular its relation to the National Curriculum provides a context for subsequent chapters but it is important that both school librarians and teachers are aware of both the school context and the wider educational context of the developments of IT in schools. Keeping up to date with initiatives and examples of good practice across the country is a vital issue for both professions. School librarians in particular have a responsibility to act as information providers to themselves and to teachers in relation to new uses of IT as well as the availability of new hardware and software.

In order to justify the often large financial outlay for a range of IT hardware and software in the school, there is a need for school librarians and teachers to be able to present rational and numerate arguments to senior school management. These arguments will be based firmly on the educational use of IT in the library and in the classroom. Schools now have much more sophisticated database systems which can be exploited to improve pupils' learning skills and use of resources. Developing these databases and linking this development to extending pupils' skills in information use is a key role for schools. Employers continually stress that they are looking for personnel who can not only use a computer but can effectively *use* information as the basis for teamwork and decision-making.

The use of online information and information retrieved from CD-ROMs is now widespread in UK schools. Both provide pupils with access to previously undreamt-of sources and amounts of information. In order that these sources do not overwhelm pupils, teachers are linking the use of these sources with curriculum-based assignments and stressing the need for pupils to identify clearly the purpose of information searches before using online or CD-ROM sources.

The chapter on selecting software provides a focus for both school librarians and teachers by highlighting the need for an interchange of information not only about sources of information on learning resources but the need to identify clearly the *curricular* use of IT resources before ordering them for the school. Inservice training for school librarians is very patchy across the country but one trend identified is the need for joint INSET for both librarians and teachers, who have a common purpose in schools.

The future of IT in schools promises startling changes in the capacity of hardware and sophistication of software. The role of both the teacher and the librarian (and perhaps the school itself) will change as technology becomes more able to carry out some of the functions presently performed by school staff. Change must be expected and the schools which have welcomed changes in IT and exploited these changes have been rewarded by improvements in quality.

It is hoped that this book will provide both an educational rationale for, as well as practical examples of the use of, IT across the curriculum in schools. The use of IT-based learning resources in the curriculum is not featured strongly in many books on IT in schools and the role of the school librarian is often underrated. If this book can serve to foster the development of IT in schools and help to encourage teachers and school librarians to work together for educational ends, it will have served its purpose.

References
1   Carter, C. and Monaco, J., *Learning information technology skills*, British Library, 1987.
2   Herring, J. E. (ed.), *The microcomputer, the school librarian and the teacher*, Bingley, 1987.

1 Information technology in schools: the context

James E. Herring

Introduction

All secondary schools in the UK now have some microcomputers available for use by teachers and pupils. In some schools, the use of information technology is taken for granted in virtually all subjects, and pupils are accustomed to using library information systems to find references to educational resources of various kinds – books, periodical articles, videos and tape-slide packages. They are also accustomed to using CD-ROM to search for full-text information and perhaps have the opportunity to search for up-to-date full-text information online. In other schools, using a microcomputer is still a rare experience for pupils and an even rarer one for all but a few teachers. In between these two extremes are schools at various stages of development. Some schools have carefully worked out information technology strategies and are frustrated by the lack of money to achieve their ideal solutions. Some schools, particularly in the independent sector, do not suffer from lack of money but do not have the staff or the policies to introduce widespread use of IT across the curriculum.

Certain trends can be isolated. There are now fewer schools with little information technology provision and as the cost of hardware becomes relatively cheaper, the numbers of microcomputers – PC compatibles, Nimbus, Apple Macintosh, Archimedes and BBC – in schools will definitely grow and perhaps the majority of schools in the UK will progress towards the target of one microcomputer for every twelve pupils set by the National Association of Advisers in Computer Education within the next three to five years.[1] The number of computers in a school, however, does not determine the quality of usage. In educational terms, microcomputer hardware and software are similar to all other learning resources. For example, a school library with 30,000 books, audiovisual and computer based resources is not necessarily a better educational resource than a library with only 10,000 items. The key factors are the use made of the educational resources and the quality of staff – teachers and school librarians – managing those resources.

The aim of this chapter is to provide teachers and school librarians with a context into which the use of information technology in the library and in the classroom and the development of information skills can be placed. A holistic view of how IT is affecting the teaching and learning process in schools is important if the focus on learning resources in subsequent chapters is to be placed in the context of the school curriculum as a whole and the totality of the use of IT in schools. This chapter will examine the use of information technology in schools in relation to the National Curriculum; the debate over the IT curriculum; the learning and teaching of information skills; the use of hardware and software in different areas of the curriculum; and the roles of the teacher and the school librarian in improving and extending the curricular use of IT in schools.

The National Curriculum[2]

In relation to the use of information technology in schools, a major change came about when the National Curriculum clearly stated that pupils should have a right to participate in a curriculum which involved the use of IT. The National Curriculum (in England and Wales) produced minimum requirements for the availability of IT in the curriculum and also highlighted different curricular areas which should take responsibility for covering particular aspects of IT. The National Curriculum also stresses that each school should be able to offer pupils full exposure to IT-related learning experiences and prepare a coherent programme for pupils which avoids duplication in different curricular subjects. The use of information technology in schools is thus now a statutory requirement for all schools, as the statutory orders published for subjects include references to information technology, while the Technology orders indicate separate attainment targets for IT. Thus a major challenge is faced by secondary schools, especially in relation to the effective cross-curricular use of computers in schools.

The National Curriculum documents require that the school curriculum must ensure that a pupil 'has the opportunity to use information technology where its use is helpful to his or her task'. The emphasis here is on allowing pupils to use the most appropriate software within subjects, e.g. word processing in English or data-gathering software in Science. It is also expected that a pupil will use information technology 'to enhance and enrich his or her learning in every area of the curriculum'. As will be seen below, there are major problems in achieving such a standard in most schools.

The use of information technology, according to the National

Curriculum, can provide pupils with new ways of dealing with difficult topics. For example, software packages such as DEVELOPING TRAY can be used in English to help with difficult texts and word-processing software can allow pupils to concentrate on the content of their work and not merely its presentation. IT should also ensure that each pupil 'has the scope of their learning potential extended by the appropriate use of IT'. This would include the use of simulation packages in Science or packages which model the economy in Business Studies.

Pupils should not only know how to use information technology in various subject areas but should also appreciate the implications of technological developments for society, e.g. in relation to employment, leisure or the home. The ethical implications of using information technology to store and disseminate personal information should also be studied.

The National Curriculum defines the ability which each pupil should have by stating that pupils should use information technology to:

communicate and handle information
design, develop, explore and evaluate models of real or imaginary
    situations
measure and control physical variables and movement.

They should be able to make informed judgements about the application and importance of information technology, and its effect on the quality of life.

This implies that pupils will have to be taught knowledge and skills in relation to a number of different aspects of IT both in school and in the outside world.

Pupils, the National Curriculum states, should have a 'coordinated and coherent programme of relevant IT experiences'. Therefore schools will have to ensure that the planning of the teaching of information technology applications is carefully calculated and that all staff in the school understand the implications of the National Curriculum requirements. Otherwise, there is the danger of having gaps or duplication in the curriculum. In a number of National Curriculum reports, it is recommended that a whole-school policy should be adopted.

In practice, as noted above, the actual implementation of the National Curriculum requirements in schools across the country is patchy, in terms of both the scope of the use of IT across the curriculum and the extent to which IT is used in particular subject areas. Government reports such as that from the Parliamentary Office of Science and Technology[3] often provide examples of the numbers of pupils using microcomputers in schools but, as Griffin and Davies note, 'As there is no reference to the duration, purpose and quality of such use, the information is of limited use'.[4] However, recommendations, such as those of the NAACE noted above, can be helpful for teachers and school librarians to use in arguments for greater provision and more quality use of information technology in their own schools.

The major implications for schools of the National Curriculum requirements relate to the ability of teachers to use information technology and the availability of relevant resources and technical support for the use of such resources, but the overriding consideration must be in relation to the teaching and learning carried out in school. Information technology should be harnessed to improve the ways in which pupils learn in schools. Griffin and Davies state that 'The aims must be for the whole curriculum to be relevant and for children to be encouraged to become life long learners, able to tackle the learning process with a high level of independence and taking account of all available resources'.[5]

Thus the approach to IT in schools, in the classroom and in the library must be taken from the stance that it is the education of the pupils which must be considered first and the resources (IT or otherwise) to support this learning should then be considered.

In Scotland, where the National Curriculum does not apply, there is a similar pattern regarding the growing use of information technology across the curriculum. The importance of the 'learning first/technology second' approach is highlighted by McDonald, who quotes a Scottish Education Department report as stating that 'the important thing for the majority of teachers will be to concentrate on the planning of the learning and teaching process and the technology will fall naturally into place'.[6]

The IT curriculum or IT across the curriculum?

The view taken by the National Curriculum that the most educationally effective method of encouraging pupils to make use of information technology is to ensure that IT is used across the whole curriculum, is viewed by most teachers as an excellent vision but one which is limited at present by the realities of today's schools. These realities include the need for better training for teachers; the need for the appointment of IT coordinators in schools and the need to extend the IT-based resources, both hardware and software, in schools.

There has been a continuing debate in the 1980s and 1990s between the notions of a coherent but pervasive IT curriculum or that of a more restricted foundation-level IT curriculum. Writers such as Evans[7] and Birnbaum[8] supported the notion of basic information technology courses in the early years of secondary schools along with the creation of IT modules which could be taught in other areas of the curriculum. The argument put forward to support these ideas is that if information technology is introduced in various subjects, it will be difficult to avoid wide differences in the quality of teaching and the learning acquired by pupils, as these might relate more to the IT knowledge of the individual teacher as opposed to his/her own subject knowledge.

Allen argues that the prerequisites for a coherent approach to IT across the curriculum are that 'a school must have a fully committed senior school management team and a coordinator with appropriate powers'.[9] There should also be, Allen states, a written programme of the pupils' IT experiences across various subjects and a coherence which ensures that all departments identify with this programme. Linked to this overall programme should be an assessment schedule, carried out by subject teachers, who may, however, have little experience in assessing the new areas relating to IT as identified by the National Curriculum. A further difficulty is the ever-changing nature of IT in schools and in society in general. Allen argues that this continuing change could have a destabilizing effect on schools and that 'The changes may simply be too much for the curriculum to handle. In this situation, there would, in the short term at least, be a need to define a clearly defined set of IT experiences in order to keep the changes it causes in perspective and undermine the instability it might cause.'[10]

The reality in most schools in the UK at present is that pupils' experiences of using IT tend to occur in the early years of secondary education in courses designed specifically to introduce pupils to different applications of computer technology, IT applications and the social impact of information technology. The advantages of such courses are that they ensure that all pupils have a basic grounding in applications such as word processing, simple databases and desktop publishing. Such courses also concentrate resources in a specific area of the school, thereby ensuring continuous use; avoid the need for large-scale in-service training (INSET) for teachers not familiar with IT; and concentrate IT assessment in areas where the teachers doing the assessment are familiar with the subject. The major drawback of courses such as these is the tendency to ghetto-ize IT, thereby restricting both the pupils' and the non-IT subject teachers' vision of the potential of IT across the curriculum. The major problem faced by schools today is that IT applications in subject areas often occur haphazardly and are due mainly to the knowledge or enthusiasm of particular teachers. The problem is magnified when such teachers leave a school and little or no training has been given to other teachers in relation to the IT applications.

The issue of INSET for IT within schools is a vital area. This was highlighted clearly in the HMI report on information technology in schools, which stated, under a section entitled 'Issues for school management', that 'Suitable inservice training is crucial to success in an area like IT, which evolves so rapidly. While some teachers regularly exploit the potential of IT in their subject many lack the necessary confidence and expertise'.[11]

HMI also stress the need for school working parties to face the training issue and identify areas of need within the school. The membership of such working parties should include teachers with IT expertise, a teacher responsible for IT across the curriculum and a member of senior management who 'should have oversight of all aspects of resources for learning, including IT and the library'.[12] Without adequate training and encouragement, it is unlikely that individual subject teachers will be able to appreciate how IT could improve their own classroom practice and help to enhance the learning experiences of pupils in different curricular subjects. Subject teachers may tend to take the view that coping with the changes in their subject as demanded by the National Curriculum restricts the amount of time they might devote to learning about IT. As will be seen below, the role of the school librarian could help to alleviate some of the worries which teachers have.

The key issue in relation to IT in the curriculum is not information technology but the curriculum itself and issues concerning learning and teaching. Somekh and Davies argue that:

> Computers, of themselves, are not transforming. Pedagogy is the focus for curricular action: it is the process by which teachers effect the development of knowledge, in its widest definitions, in learners. The development of a pedagogy for IT is the process whereby we learn to interrelate creatively with computers in educational events. The machine becomes an expression of human endeavour and growth; its opportunities are exploited, it is not in control.[13]

The findings of the PALM project clearly show that IT can assist in developing pupil autonomy in learning but in order for this to be achieved, pupils need to work in an environment conducive to learning and teachers need to re-examine their classroom role in relation to IT.

Thus the issues of learning, teaching, INSET and the availability of IT resources are inseparable and it will be those schools who face these issues as a whole that will succeed in going towards the ideals set out by the National Curriculum.

IT and information skills

The work done by Marland and others in producing *Information skills in the secondary curriculum*[14] has formed the basis for most studies on information skills in the past ten years. Projects looking specifically at information skills and the use of information technology include the Microcomputer in the School Library Project (MISLIP),[15] and Carter and Monaco's 'Learning information technology skills' project.[16] Both projects sought to discover whether particular skills were needed to use computer-based sources of information or whether the same skills applied whatever the medium being used to find and use information.

Carter and Monaco used the findings of Marland *et al.* and grouped the key information skills into five areas:

1) FORMULATING and ANALYSING the information need (What have I got to do?)
2) RETRIEVING information relevant to that need (How do I get the information I need?)
3) PROCESSING that information (What should I record?)
4) COMMUNICATING the information (How should I present the information?)
5) EVALUATING the information and the task undertaken (Have I got all the information I need? What have I achieved from undertaking this task?)[17]

The main findings of the project were that pupils were in general poor at step 1. This was partly due to the fact that pupils were not made sufficiently aware of the importance of this step and that teachers often assumed that the task was well designed and would encourage a sense of enquiry in the pupils. There was also a lack of direction given to pupils in terms of retrieving information and they often failed to have a search strategy prepared when using computer-based sources. Higher-ability pupils were better at skimming and scanning information retrieved but many pupils had problems in this area. The technology itself did not prove to be a motivating factor for pupils in finding information. In MISLIP, the findings were that pupils using library databases *were* motivated by using computer-based sources as opposed to the traditional library catalogue. Pupils were motivated in the Carter and Monaco project by using IT to communicate information but were poor at evaluating what had been done. A particularly interesting conclusion from this study is that 'In all the above observations, it was not usually the technology *per se* that caused problems but a lack of awareness and application of information skills'.[18]

The above studies confirm the importance of information skills for pupil learning and also stress the need for both teachers and librarians to be aware of what is involved in teaching information skills and to understand the importance of motivating pupils to apply the skills in their curricular work. Carter and Monaco state clearly that 'individual teachers/librarians could not work successfully in isolation, and the involvement of, and/or support from other members of staff appeared crucial to pupil acceptance of both the individuals and their teaching'.[19]

The introduction of the National Curriculum served to strengthen the hand of those teachers and school librarians involved in teaching information skills in schools. In Key Stages 3 and 4, it is clear from Statements of Attainment and Programme of Study Statements in various areas of the curriculum that information skills are seen as vital components of a pupil's overall learning skills. In many schools, where lip service had been paid to information skills before the arrival of the National Curriculum, teachers in particular are now much more conscious of the need to teach these skills across the curriculum, in relation to the use of information technology resources as well as print or audiovisual resources. Figure 1.1 shows a sample of information skills statements from National Curriculum Key Stages 3 and 4.

What can be clearly seen from Figure 1.1 is that while pupils using information technology may have to learn new mechanical skills such as how to load software, follow instructions within the package, and save and print information, these skills are low-level skills which pupils will learn easily. The more complex skills lie in the pupil's ability to identify need, to gather, evaluate and effectively use information. The information retrieved from a CD-ROM or online database or pupil-created database is no different from information found in textbooks and periodical articles. It may be more up to date and it may be in greater detail or be better illustrated but unless pupils have ability in the information skills noted above, they will not benefit from the technological advances through which IT can provide pupils with much greater access to *potentially* relevant information. The information will only become *actually* relevant if it is used to meet the needs of the pupils' requirements. Thus the greater use of information technology to allow pupils to retrieve a wider variety of information makes the teaching of information skills more important in today's schools.

Key Stage 3
Pupils should
● analyse and interpret data from complex secondary sources (for example, from a Census database) **Geography AT8**
● have opportunities to produce writing and proof-read on a word processor **English AT3 4 5 POS**
● begin to use, with increasing confidence, information and data accessed from a computer **Science POS**
● organize and express results of historical study . . . for example, by creating a database **History POS**
● use IT to combine and organize different forms of information for a presentation to an audience **Technology AT5**
● select and interrogate a computer database to obtain information needed for a task **Technology AT5**

Key Stage 4
Pupils should
● design successful means of collecting information for computer processing **Technology AT5**
● define the information required, the purposes for which it is needed and how it will be analysed; and to take these things into account in designing ways of collecting and organizing information when creating a database **Technology AT5 POS**
● use information-handling software to capture, store, retrieve, analyse and present information **Technology AT5 POS**
● evaluate methods of searching and storing data manually and using a computer **Technology AT5 POS**
● be able to select an appropriate piece of data management software to perform a particular task in data storage and retrieval **Science AT12**

Fig. 1.1

IT applications

It is not possible to highlight all the actual and potential applications of information technology in the secondary curriculum, but by using some of the classifications adopted in the HMI report above, it is possible to show the *variety* of IT applications across the curriculum.

Art

The report states that pupils studying Art should 'Use IT to support existing art and design media, as well as to generate imagery'. There are many art packages available for the different microcomputers used in schools. Software such as PAINTBRUSH for PC compatibles allows pupils to create pictures using different-sized brushes, rubber banding with firm, dashed and dotted lines, spray, fill, text and snap to grid facilities. IMAGINE for the Archimedes range extends the possible options open to pupils by allowing them to manipulate two colour screens at one time and to copy portions of a picture from one screen to another. IMAGINE could also be used in Maths as it has a wide range of shape-drawing routines, as well as routines for difficult skills such as mapping and symmetry.

English

HMI argue that, in English, pupils should 'Use IT to help in the generation of both written (prose and verse) and spoken language'. The use of word-processing and desktop publishing software in English is now extremely common. The use of packages such as NEWSNET allows pupils to create newspapers in a real-life simulation. NEWSNET allows pupils to participate in the creation of a real newspaper by taking on the roles of journalists, sub-editors and newsroom editors. The package is an integrated one, containing three databases for research, a word-processing facility, an electronic mail simulation, a digitised picture library and a desktop publishing unit to bring all the material together. NEWSNET and similar packages were used in the Microcomputers in Curriculum English (MICE) project which identified a range of benefits to pupils in 'problem solving and collaborative writing . . . drafting and language awareness. Reading skills, especially skimming and scanning . . . listening and talking in a variety of forms'.[20]

Geography

HMI state that, in Geography, pupils should 'Explore computer based simulations of geographical phenomena'. There is a wide range of geographical software now available in schools, covering different aspects of the Geography curriculum, e.g. physical geography. The National Council for Educational Technology (NCET) produced the Learning Geography with Computers Pack[21] which includes a number of software packages such as STARS where pupils compete with each other as petrol station managers in order to gain maximum profit. CHOOSING SITES, from the same pack, asks pupils to analyse the factors involved in land use, one of which is the location of a new car plant in the UK. SANDHARVEST provides pupils with a realistic and up-to-date simulation of life in real villages in Mali. This software includes elements of the impact of political decisions on agriculture as well as aspects relating to the life of ordinary women in villages. Such simulations can broaden the knowledge of pupils as well as stimulating them to ask questions about Third World countries.

Mathematics

HMI expect pupils studying Maths to 'Use sensibly numerical, algebraic, graphical and programmable calculators, and a spreadsheet facility'. The use of spreadsheets by pupils has potential applications in a number of subject areas such as CDT, Geography and History, but pupils need to understand the statistical concepts involved in using spreadsheets before they can fully appreciate such applications in other subjects. DATASHEET for the Archimedes is a spreadsheet specifically designed for use in education. The spreadsheet contains 200 rows by 20 columns which can handle numbers, text and formulae. Output from DATASHEET can be to a printer or data can be saved as an ACSII file which can be imported into a word-processing or desktop publishing package. This allows pupils to present statistical data in reports or projects.

Music
HMI state that, in Music, pupils should 'Use IT with discrimination to compose, manipulate, refine and produce music of quality'. The use of IT in the Music curriculum has been greatly hampered by the costs involved in buying hardware and software but, as these costs have been reduced recently, there is now more opportunity to exploit IT in the Music curriculum. In Hurlingham and Chelsea School, Ringer reports that the use of synthesizers and software such as PRO PERFORMER for the Apple Macintosh allowed pupils to 'harness technology to make music' but adds significantly that in the Music curriculum 'IT is there as a servicing agency, not to lead the activity'. The use of such software has not only allowed pupils to create music in a more sophisticated environment but has also greatly enhanced pupils' skills in discussion, problem-solving and cooperation. Pupils at the school are also encouraged to evaluate what they have done and also to evaluate the role of the computer as an aid to their work.[22]

The above examples provide a small sample of the use of educational software in secondary schools and indicate a range of skills that pupils can acquire through using IT. In all of the above examples, where software is used, it is not the only learning resource used by pupils. In the schools using NEWSNET, for example, pupils made extensive use of books, newspapers and periodicals to support the work done on projects. What is clear is that, if used properly and in conjunction with other learning resources, IT can improve the learning skills of pupils.

The role of the teacher and the school librarian
As noted above in relation to information skills and as will be demonstrated in the following chapters, the importance of staff in schools working together to enhance the use of information

technology in schools, cannot be underestimated. From the headteacher downwards, all staff in a school should be aware of the requirements of the National Curriculum, both in relation to their own subjects, but also across the curriculum. In this respect, school librarians have a role in providing teachers with up-to-date information on IT and the National Curriculum requirements by alerting them to new DES reports, articles in *The Times educational supplement* or in other educational journals. Both teachers and school librarians wishing to see their schools at the forefront of IT use, should ensure that there is pressure put on senior school management to set up working parties on IT and information skills across the curriculum, in order to produce whole-school policies.

School librarians are in a position to have an overview of curricular developments in the various subject areas in school and part of their role could be to work with teachers on projects involving IT use and the development of information skills and to act as a catalyst between departments, so that not only do different departments know what their colleagues are doing but also departments can learn from each other's use of IT. CD-ROM is an excellent example of a cross-curricular resource (as will be seen in a later chapter), and sources such as the electronic encyclopedias can be used by different teachers as part of project work for pupils in different areas of the curriculum. Part of the role of the school librarian will be to inform teachers as a whole how individual teachers have used the resource, for what purposes and with what success. The teachers may provide the basis for joint reports to senior management on the use of such resources.

Inservice training both for teachers and school librarians has been noted as a vital area. The cascade method, whereby, for example, a History teacher attends a course on using Census databases and returns to teach colleagues in the school, is a well-proven method of in-school INSET which can involve both teachers (and not only History teachers) and school librarians. A useful role to be played by school librarians is to serve as the main source of information (perhaps held on a database) of which teachers are attending IT-related courses and what knowledge has been gained. Other teachers may then be motivated either to attend courses themselves or to learn from those teachers who have been on courses. School librarians who attend courses run by their local school library services on topics like CD-ROM should also use the cascade method to inform teachers about the courses attended.

Conclusion
It can be seen from this overview of IT in schools that change is

constant and that the pressures on school staff are enormous. Change can be destabilizing or it can be a motivating factor. The key factor in educational change tends to be the attitudes of the staff involved. If teachers and school librarians can demonstrate that developments in IT and in information skills teaching and learning can act to improve the learning environment for pupils and improve the teaching environment for teachers, then changes may be seen as stimulating. If they can show that the introduction of more sophisticated hardware and software into schools is done to serve the needs of the curriculum and is not done merely to keep up to date with other schools or to satisfy the needs of a few IT enthusiasts, then IT can be seen as a truly *educational* resource in schools.

References

1 *Times educational supplement*, 8 March 1991.
2 Department of Education and Science, *Technology in the National Curriculum*, HMSO, 1990.
3 *Times educational supplement*, 8 March 1991.
4 Griffin, J. A. and Davies, S.,'IT in the National Curriculum', *Journal of computer assisted learning*, **6**, 1990, 258.
5 ibid., 261.
6 McDonald, S., 'IT in the National Curriculum: the view from Scotland', *Journal of computer assisted learning*, **7**, 1991, 39.
7 Evans, N., *The future of the microcomputer in schools*, Macmillan Education, 1986.
8 Birnbaum, I., *The place of information technology in the secondary curriculum*, MUSE, 1986.
9 Allen, J. P., 'Information technology across the curriculum', *Computer education* Jun. 1991, 21.
10 ibid., 22.
11 Department of Education and Science, *Information technology from 5 to 16*, HMSO, 1989, 33.
12 ibid.
13 Somekh, B. and Davies, R., 'Towards a pedagogy for information technology', *The curriculum journal*, **2** (2), Summer 1991, 153–4.
14 Marland, M. (ed.), *Information skills in the secondary curriculum*, Methuen Educational, 1981.
15 Williams, D., 'Database creation', in Herring, J. E. (ed.), *The microcomputer, the school librarian and the teacher*, Bingley, 1987.
16 Carter, C. and Monaco, J., *Learning information technology skills*, British Library, 1987.
17 ibid., 2.
18 ibid., 5.
19 ibid., 8.
20 Preston, C., 'Reading the news', *Educational computing and technology*, **13** (2), February 1992.
21 NCET, *Learning geography with computers pack*, NCET, 1990.
22 *Times educational supplement*, update: Computers, November 1991.

2 Making a case for IT in the school library

James E. Herring

This chapter aims to provide ideas and guidelines for those schools wishing to introduce elements of information technology into the school library as well as for those schools who wish to extend their library IT provision in order to widen the scope for information use in the library and the classroom. All schools will have their own particular structures in terms of financial decision-making and IT policy-making but the basic mechanisms for arguing a case for the acquisition of new hardware and software in the library, and justifying that acquisition on educational terms, will be similar in most schools. The most usual method used to make a case for IT provision is to prepare a report, which can be verbal but will probably be in written form, for the headteacher or a school committee which deals with resources. In this chapter suggestions as to the shape of such a report, its content and who might draft and present the report, will be provided. Examples from schools who have gone through this process, some at the basic level of introducing microcomputers into the library for the first time and others at a more advanced level, will be used as sources of inspiration for teachers and school librarians, rather than as documents to be copied verbatim.

It is worthwhile looking at what a report should achieve before discussing its content. In her book *Report writing*,[1] Booth states that certain decisions have to be made when writing a report, including the following:

(a) the *purpose* for which it is being written
(b) the specific *topic*
(c) the precise *message* to be delivered
(d) the appropriate *structure*
(e) suitable *length* and *format*
(f) the right *vocabulary*, *style* and *tone*
(g) the amount and kind of supporting *evidence* and *data*.

The purpose of the report will be to justify the inclusion or extension of IT provision in the school library on educational grounds. This is important as the school's decision-makers may have little knowledge of the use of IT for information retrieval and information use. Despite the growth in the literature on IT in schools, the emphasis in most books on IT use in schools still relates to computer studies applications and computer-assisted learning (CAL). The report will therefore try to extend the knowledge of the school's management in relation to IT use in the school library.

The report will also be a vehicle for convincing the school's hierarchy of the need to devote extra finance to information resources in the library, since these resources will be available to the school as a whole, will be directly relevant to the school curriculum and will not merely be additions to the traditional library tools.

The report may also be attempting to introduce new approaches to existing work in the curriculum, which will have implications for the use of resources both in the library and in the classroom, for teaching methods presently used in the school and for the information skills pupils will use in identifying the purpose of, finding and using information in their curricular work. If this is one of the aims of the report, it will have to be carefully worded, if it is not to appear controversial.

The main aim of the report will be to convince those controlling finance that the new venture will support existing facilities and provide added value in the form of new resources which will support teachers and pupils by providing new opportunities for improving learning and teaching in the school.

Prerequisites

Before actually writing the report, the school librarian and teachers involved in its compilation will have to consider certain factors relating to its content as well as the consequences of submitting it. One consequence to be considered is that the report's authors may have to answer questions relating to the report at committee meetings in the school. An important consideration here is terminology. The report will cover hardware and software requirements as well as the uses to be made of the new resources (e.g. a CD-ROM system). The school librarian and teachers may have to anticipate questions on the efficiency of the system, such as whether there will be a need for expansion of the system in the future, or on the capacity of the software, such as the number of records which can be handled by a database. There may also be questions about the limitations of the hardware and software, for example whether the hardware is compatible with existing microcomputers in the school or whether the software can be networked.

An important factor here will be the school librarian's experience of using the hardware and software required. One of the difficulties faced by both teachers and school librarians is the need to cope with new hardware in particular. This will be the case either when the librarian or teachers have little experience of using IT or when (e.g. with CD-ROM) the hardware being used is outside the previous experience of the school staff. Thus before the report is submitted, the school librarian should gain some experience of using the new hardware and software. This can be done either through the local school library service or by visiting another school which already has the relevant hardware and software. Visits to schools who have already acquired systems, for example integrated library systems, are invaluable in that the experience of the school librarian and teachers already using the hardware and software can be tapped. Questions can be asked not only about the technical aspects, such as how to set up the CD-ROM system, but also about the curricular use of the new resource: which subject areas have used the new resource most?; what need was there for training for pupils and/or teachers to use the new resource?; what evaluation has been carried out?; and what problems have arisen since the new hardware and software were acquired?

It is important that the school librarian should feel confident in demonstrating the potential of the hardware and software to be acquired as this may be requested by senior staff before a commitment is made to provide finance. Because the application may be new to the school, the school librarian and teachers involved in the report will want to impress senior staff by their ability not only to use the hardware and software but also to explain its potential use in the curriculum.

Once suitable experience has been gained, a plan for the report can be drawn up. In schools which have most successfully exploited IT in the school library, justification for new resources has usually been based initially on a specific educational project, managed by both school librarian and teachers. The project should be shown to be something which can be integrated into the school's curricular work and can enhance pupils' learning skills, and not a project solely based on library work or solely aimed at showing pupils how to use the library, although this may be part of the project.

The project should be discussed by the school librarian and the teachers to examine the following:

(a) what is being taught
(b) what skills pupils are expected to acquire
(c) what aspects of information handling are involved

(d) at what stage of the project pupils will use IT

(e) what information pupils will gain from using IT resources and how this information will be used.

In Solihull Sixth-Form College (SSFC) (see also Chapter 5), the need to justify the growing provision of IT is a constant one and both the librarian and the teachers involved are urged to see the justification for IT as part of the development of the school's IT policy. The setting up of a new online service in the library required a case to be made and this included anticipating counter-arguments and having a clear idea of the management and administrative implications.

The advent of more formal or structured planning processes in schools encouraged by initiatives such as Local Management of Schools (LMS) can give school librarians and teachers the opportunity to express the need for development of library services as part of the overall school plan. The planning process is a continuous one with a cycle of analysis of the present situation, proposals for future development, implementation of proposals and evaluation of the action taken. In SSFC, therefore, the planning for the new online service had to be placed in this overall context as part of the library development plan and the whole school development plan.

Schools have produced a range of documents to aid the planning process and it is important that the library is seen to be integrated with other departments in the planning process. Thus any plan for new IT facilities in the library, such as online services at SSFC, will necessarily have to fit in with the plans of teaching departments, and one element of the justification for new IT resources will be how the new resources will support the plans of subject departments.

Some school librarians see the school development plan as an ideal opportunity for school librarians to become more involved in the management processes of the school curriculum and to ensure that the library is considered in the overall plan. Justification of library IT developments, involving initial purchase of IT equipment for the library or the development of existing resources, will involve analysis of curriculum need, projected potential and costings for all implications of change. A report on IT developments will also have to demonstrate the management and administrative implications of any changes to be made and what performance criteria may be used to measure the success of the project. Figure 2.1 shows a document used at SSFC by all staff in the college and used by the librarian and teachers as part of the justification for new IT resources in the library.

Context for planning: POLICIES
I.T.
Curriculum
Staff development
School and LEA priorities
FINANCIAL AWARENESS

Possible sources:

Capitation
TVE
Parents
Local initiatives
Government initiatives
Local companies
Other, e.g. TECs

What are likely to be other major demands?

KNOWLEDGE AND UNDERSTANDING OF:
- the procedures, structures and processes in the school for planning
- the people to influence and persuade
- any informal channels of influence
- who may be likely to support
- who will benefit
- what others are doing

Fig. 2.1

Other guidelines used at SSFC are shown in Figures 2.2 and 2.3. These forms could be used by a group preparing a report and could be particularly useful if completed by different members of the group and then the completed forms used to collate ideas about a possible report being prepared.

Audit and Analysis Sheet
(for construction of rationale and plan)

Proposal:

Experience:

Know:

Lessons learned:

Need to know:

How to find out:

Want to achieve:

Who will benefit:

Fig. 2.2

Plan construction

Proposal:
Who?
Where?
How? and when?
Implications:

- training:
- administration:
- associated resources:
other:

Estimated costs:
(details and information to be attached)

Fig. 2.3

Another technique which is commonly used in management contexts to plan reports is 'SWOT' analysis. This technique was used at SSFC in relation to the introduction of online information services in the library and the resulting discussions identified the following conclusions:

Strengths
  Immediacy
  Up to date
  Wide-ranging information sources
  'Real-world' information sources – found in business and higher
    education
  Information is relevant to curriculum
  Able to cope with unpredictable information requests
  Helps develop information-seeking skills
  Helps develop information-handling skills

Weaknesses
  Costing difficult
  Needs dedicated phone-line
  Search procedures differ
  Needs an intermediary
  Searches need very careful preparation
  Will consume staff time
  Will consume paper and disks

Opportunities
  Gives pupils experience of how information is handled in commercial world
  Gives the library a high profile
  Increases links with departments
  Can get library closely involved with pupils' work and with course planning

Threats
  May suggest that other sources of information are redundant
  May create hostility among the computer-shy

A SWOT analysis will not provide a complete overview of the project under consideration but can raise valuable ideas which can be discussed by the school librarian and teachers who are putting a proposal forward.

Using some of the ideas above, a 'model' report justifying the acquisition of a CD-ROM facility in the school library might contain the following elements:

Title: IT resources and the school curriculum
Project: To explore the curricular use of newspapers on CD-ROM with particular regard to Year 8 Geography and History.
Staff: D White (Geography), K Wright (History), J Anderson (School Librarian)

Aims:
  To examine the use of the *Times/Sunday Times* CD-ROM as a curricular resource in Year 8 Geography and History
  To develop pupils' information skills in the classroom and in the library

Objectives:
  (1) To improve pupils' ability in planning project work
  (2) To introduce pupils to CD-ROM technology
  (3) To extend pupils' ability to search for and find relevant information using a full-text electronic source of information
  (4) To improve pupils' ability to use effectively information retrieved from CD-ROM and other sources of information in the library and in the classroom

Methodology:
Pupils in Year 8 Geography will be studying aspects of pollution in the environment. Pupils will work in groups, examining a particular aspect of pollution which has been discussed by the teacher and the group. Pupils will be expected to identify the information they need before using the library and will use SEARCH worksheets which have been designed by

the project group. Pupils will search the CD-ROM for up-to-date information as well as using other sources in the library.

Pupils in Year 8 History will study aspects of political change in Europe and how these changes are reported in the *Times/Sunday Times*. The pupils will compare the up-to-date reports with copies of reports (available in class) from late 19th-century newspapers. Part of this project will also be covered in the pupils' English curriculum. Pupils will work in groups and plan searches for information on topics agreed with the teacher. As with Geography, pupils will use the SEARCH worksheets.

In both subject areas, pupils will be expected to work together to identify relevant keywords which they will use when searching the CD-ROM and using other library resources. There will be an emphasis on the pupils' ability to identify the purpose of, find and use effectively information *both* in the classroom *and* in the library. Pupils will incorporate results of searches into their projects but will also be expected to paraphrase reports found.

Hardware
An IBM compatible PC (e.g. Nimbus) with CD-ROM drive plus a printer (**Note** – a bid for this equipment is currently being made under TVEI)

Software
Times/Sunday Times CD-ROM disk

Costs
Hardware £
Software £
Total: £

Timescale:
The Geography project will run in term 1 and the History project in term 2 of next session.

Evaluation
The projects will be evaluated with particular attention being paid to:

(1) The ability of pupils to improve the planning of their project work
(2) The effectiveness of discussion sessions between pupil groups and the teacher in helping pupils to define their topics
(3) The ability of pupils to identify *relevant* keywords and their use of the SEARCH worksheets
(4) The role of the school librarian as facilitator in pupils' work in the library
(5) The pupils' ability to use CD-ROM as an effective information resource
(6) The value of pre-planning sessions involving the teachers and the school librarian

A report will be presented in term 3 of next session. The report may form the basis of articles for publication in relevant geography, history and library periodicals.

D. White, K. Wright, J. Anderson

Presenting such a report obviously does not guarantee success, and the politics of the particular school will be an important factor in relation to such a report. The teachers, for example, will need the backing of their department heads and the project group may be advised to try to obtain support from the member of the senior management team in the school responsible for resources. As will be seen from the examples below, the *methods* used to gain support for the project will vary from school to school, but the basic arguments will remain similar. The project team may also be advised to talk to colleagues in other departments who could run similar projects in the future. The Economics teachers, for example, would be able to use the *Times* CD-ROM to allow pupils to use the financial sections of the paper in their coursework. The school librarian can also back up the case for the report by having information on the range of other CD-ROM products available and how these might be used in the curriculum.

Obtaining agreement for the purchase of relatively expensive IT hardware and software in the school library will not be an easy task for teachers and school librarians, but the main lessons to be learned from those school librarians who have successfully justified the acquisition of IT resources in the library can be summed up as follows:

(1) School librarians and teachers must present joint reports.
(2) The *educational* rationale for purchasing the hardware and software must be most prominent in the report.
(3) The report should be presented in a professional manner and backed up by other evidence not in the report.

Examples

Durham Johnson Comprehensive School
This is an example of a school moving from a situation where there was no IT provision in the library to the integration of library resources (including IT) with the curriculum. This example shows not only the basis of the proposal to senior management within the school but also the different stages of negotiation needed to put the proposal into practice.

Proposal

Aims
> To develop the school library into 'a central powerhouse of learning, continually consulted by pupils of all ages'

To extend the use of IT across the curriculum
To provide a central base for IT in the school
To examine the exploitation of IT in the school library

Objectives

(1) To extend the present upper site library by incorporating the landing area, adjacent to the library, into the library
(2) To develop the use of IT resources within the library for the benefit of the school as a whole by introducing into the library:

    (a) a network of 15 microcomputers;
    (b) an integrated library system (Micro Librarian) to facilitate keywording of resources and enhanced information retrieval;
    (c) CD-ROM facility to allow pupils to search full-text electronic media

(3) To enhance pupils' information skills through the introduction of IT-based information sources

Funding
TVEI funding has been identified which will cover the costs of the IT hardware and software required. Conversion of currently unused space and purchase of new furniture to house IT resources would be covered within school funds. Detailed costs of IT hardware and software and of internal furnishings are listed separately.

Proposed benefits
The school will have a library which will be a centre for learning and a key curricular resource in the school
Pupils will have access to up-to-date electronic media which they will exploit within their curricular work
Greater use of the library by staff and pupils will more fully exploit print-based information resources in the library
A central IT resource base will provide support to departmentally based IT resources
The use of IT across the curriculum will be greatly enhanced by the library development

The process
The above proposal represents an amalgam of different documents and verbal reports presented at different committees within the school. The key stages in the proposal being accepted were as follows:

Stage 1
Discussion between school librarian and TVEI coordinator (also with overall responsibility for the library) on the plans to extend the library and introduce IT.

Stage 2
Discussions between the TVEI coordinator and head of IT on a central school network based initially in the library.

Stage 3
The proposed network discussed at and supported by the school's IT Development Group who agreed that a large proportion of the school's TVEI funding should be directed towards a central IT resource area.

Stage 4
Proposals to extend the library and incorporate an IT resource area taken by TVEI coordinator to senior management meeting, which agreed that the proposal was viable.

Stage 5
The proposed library extension and siting of the network in the new library taken back to the IT Development Group by the head of IT. The group agreed to give its support.

Stage 6
The final outline plan taken to a senior management meeting by the TVEI coordinator. The meeting discussed in detail the financial implications and the implications for the curriculum and agreed to the plan.

Stage 7
Discussions between the deputy head (Finance), TVEI coordinator and the school librarian on the requirements for hardware, software and furniture purchase.

Stage 8
Discussions between head of IT and TVEI coordinator on the best use of TVEI funding to maximize the quality and quantity of resources to be purchased.

Stage 9
Implementation of original proposal and installation of new equipment and furniture.

Actual benefits
In her latest report on the library since the new developments, the school librarian identified the following benefits:

(1) Greatly increased use of the library by pupils.
(2) Extended use of the library by departments such as English, French, Maths and Science and thus more integration of the library with the curriculum.
(3) Availability of CD-ROMs – *Grolier* and *Hutchinson* encyclopedias, *World fact book*, *World atlas*, *Times/Sunday Times*, *Northern Echo* – has been a key factor in extending the use of library resources across the curriculum.
(4) More *professional* use of the school librarian's skills in relation to curriculum planning, development of information skills and the provision of INSET for teachers.

Bristol Grammar School

This example, which contains extracts from a detailed report, is a justification of the acquisition of a library management system. As will be seen below, the system is argued for not only on the grounds that it will greatly improve internal library administrative aspects such as circulation, but on *educational* grounds, particularly the improvement of information retrieval by pupils and teachers. This is also a good example of a report which identifies savings which might be made as well as the costs involved.

Proposal for a computerized library management system at BGS

The following benefits would be gained:

(1) The transfer of the library catalogue on to disk would produce a greatly enhanced system for searching for information. The power and depth of the keyword search on a computer system means that the user would be presented with far more possible sources of information at greater speed. The library is currently underused partly as a result of the difficulties of successfully accessing information through the existing card catalogue. For example, a recent request for information on the Forest of Dean, produced a list of 18 relevant resources for the teacher concerned but took a considerable amount of time. With a computerized system, a student or teacher could have entered the terms FOREST and DEAN and the 18 resources plus others would be retrieved in seconds. The student could also take away a printout of the list of resources.

At present there is no non-fiction title index – the computerized catalogue could be searched by use of title, author or subject. Also, the library could supply each head of department with a printout of books relevant to GCSE, A-level and other syllabuses by using keywords. The computer system will generate keywords from the title of resources and with the advice of teachers and pupils, we could ensure that all topics in the school curriculum were studied to produce curriculum-relevant keywords for each book or other resource. The results will be that information retrieval by pupils will be greatly enhanced and access to *all* the library resources – books, audio tapes, videos, journal articles – will be greatly improved.

Thus the advantages to subject areas across the curriculum will be seen in terms of greater use of relevant resources by pupils at all levels within the school.

(2) There would be considerable savings in library staff time once the system was established. With the present system, much time is used in processing books and producing catalogue cards. Savings will also be realized when materials are borrowed, returned and reserved.

(3) Savings in finance would result as the library would not now have to purchase a new card catalogue, which could cost over £1,000. Savings would also be made from the library fund as a result of not having to purchase readers' tickets, catalogue cards and book plates.

(4) The Dolphin system has been adopted by over 20 schools in Somerset and the schools report not only savings in staff time and in the purchase of cards etc. but also much greater use and much more *effective* use of library resources since the computerization of the library

The Chafford School
This example provides extracts from a report of an evaluation of a project which involved initial justification of the purchase of IT resources in the library. One of the aims of the project was to investigate information-handling and processing skills in approaches which gave pupils more responsibility for their own learning. Thus the development of IT resources was inextricably linked to the development of flexible learning in the school as a whole. Another aim of the project was to examine what benefits would accrue from the employment of a full-time chartered librarian in supporting the establishment of flexible learning across the curriculum. Thus the three aspects – flexible learning, IT resources and the employment of a chartered librarian – were linked as part of the educational rationale for the project.

Report on the school library project at the Chafford School, Rainham, Essex

4th year Support Group
The students quite clearly see the value of doing their curricular work with all the book and information technology resources around them.

Most now use the computers to help them with their work. This can be compared to the note recorded in a 'Record of Visit' earlier in the project which stated that 'few made much use of the library based IT facilities for a variety of reasons'.

General use of the library
Use of the library by departments has greatly increased during the period of the project. In many cases it seems to have been student-led in that staff have seen work which the students have achieved and the students themselves have asked to use the library for their work.

A group of Business Studies students made extensive use of NERIS on CD-ROM, although this resource was initially seen as a 'staff' resource.

Students have made much use of the Jobfile Explorer software on the Nimbus during their PSE lessons. Fifth-year pupils have used this resource for both work experience and actual job applications.

Staff perceptions
The Head of Chemistry has said: 'I have been surprised by how much students have enjoyed studying Chemistry in the library. They have been able to utilise the IT facilities in several collaborative ventures and this has generated a good deal of extra interest.'

First-year science (examples of work done)

9. Cooling water:	● Use of computers for graphing Producing a graph Significance of room temperature
10. Ob.15 Heating of chemicals	● Use of *databases* to record obser-vations

Classification

12. C6 – Classifying the class	● Use of IT to produce bar charts, databases of observations and then sorting or grouping

Recommendations
A full-time chartered librarian and 25 hours of clerical assistance are a minimum requirement to allow the school library to be open all through the school day and to provide support for its use as a resource-based flexible learning unit.

References

1   Booth, P. F., *Report writing*, Elm Publications, 1984.

3 Library systems

Morea Wood and Julia Allen

Introduction

As noted elsewhere in this book, the last five years have seen a major change in the type of hardware and software available to schools in general and school libraries in particular. Much of this change has been a result of a dramatic decrease in the cost of hardware but the availability of PCs with 40 – 100MB hard disks has meant that systems for school libraries, which were previously too expensive or not available in PC versions, are now within the budget of schools. Five years ago there were, for example, no suitable database systems on PCs which could hold the complete library catalogue of a school library. The systems that were available were very expensive and the methods of searching were not suited to use by pupils. In the early 1990s systems have been developed especially for schools and many systems have their own user groups across a particular LEA or in some cases, nationally. School libraries are now, in terms of systems used, becoming more like their college and university counterparts as they are increasingly seeking to automate their catalogues, their acquisition and circulation systems. Many school libraries have also invested in security systems to reduce theft. While administrative systems – circulation, acquisition and security – are valuable in themselves, the most important systems being installed in school libraries – in *educational* terms – are the database systems which allow a school to have a library catalogue which can be searched using curriculum-related keywords.

This chapter will provide an overview of available systems; a guide to selecting hardware and software; and a case study based on Cheshire schools which have found that the development of an online school library catalogue has, in some ways, transformed the way in which the school libraries' resources have been used by pupils and teachers.

Library systems

In public and academic libraries, integrated library systems such as

Plessey or GEAC have become the norm and much emphasis has been put on the effectiveness of circulation and acquisition systems as well as cataloguing systems. In schools, however, the importance of the school library catalogue as an educational tool directly linked to the school curriculum means that the efforts of school librarians and teachers will be directed mainly towards the keyworded database of learning resources. Because pupils learn more effectively by using a school library database as part of their information-seeking and information-using process, the importance of the school library catalogue becomes much greater than in other libraries. Teachers who identify curriculum-related keywords for inclusion in the database then expect pupils to use these keywords in searching for information. More importantly, teachers expect pupils to *understand* these keywords as they often represent the basis of what has been taught in the curriculum. Systems designed for school libraries, therefore, must take account of the needs of teachers and pupils.

Because of its origins within a whole-school information systems package, the most popular school library database system is the SIMS (School Information Management System) Library Management Module (see Appendix 3). The SIMS system runs on PCs under MS-DOS. It requires a hard disk with at least 40MB but, given constant updating of the system, schools would be advised to have 80–100MB of hard disk storage. The system can run on a network, providing a number of terminals within the library, or can be run on school-wide networks giving teachers and pupils access to the school library from other parts of the school. In cataloguing terms, SIMS allows up to 100 characters for a title; up to three authors; owner/location; Dewey number; date of publication; date of purchase; cost; up to 20 keywords; user-defined resource types; and facilities for multiple entries. Catalogue data may be imported from sources such as Whitaker's Bookbank on CD-ROM by using SIMS' *Libtools* package. This facility provides most of the bibliographic information needed and can radically cut down the time needed to establish a database of all school library items. Only one keyword is provided, so keywords will have to be added by the school librarian in consultation with teachers. *Libtools* also allows schools to import data from other schools or from a county database maintained by the school library service. Once the database is established, searching for pupils is available using keyword, title, author and Dewey number. The use of AND and OR to link terms facilitates searching. The quality of the output of searches will depend on the quality of the keywords used and the extent to which pupils prepare for searches before they come to the library. The database itself can help pupils by providing lists of keyword available but the *use* of keywords will have to be related to what the pupils are studying for effective searches to be made.

Other systems such as Dolphin and Heritage (see below) provide similar facilities to SIMS. Leeves and Manson's *Guide to library systems for schools*[1] is a useful guide but the market for school library systems is very fluid and careful updating of the information in this guide is advisable.

All of the systems now available for schools provide circulation components. At present, circulation systems provide school librarians with the opportunity to manage the issue, return, renewal and reservation of books and other resources either by using the keyboard or by barcoding all resources and using a light-pen for issue and return. A further advantage of using a circulation system lies in the ability of the systems to produce a variety of reports relating to use. Thus school librarians can provide teachers with reports on the use (in terms of borrowing) of different kinds of resources within the library. Thus a Geography teacher may be able to identify which resources were borrowed by a Year 9 class studying a particular part of the Geography syllabus. These reports have to be seen in the context of the 'use' of resources, i.e, they will only record use if an item has been borrowed. Many items may be consulted in the library but never borrowed. The decision on whether to use the keyboard or barcodes for issue will depend on the costs of barcoding all the stock (which can be considerable) and the ease of use of the keyboard system. As circulation in school libraries tends to be of limited volume compared with other libraries, it may be that a keyboard issue is sufficient for the library's purpose. In terms of priority, circulation will obviously come well below the provision of a keyword-based school library catalogue.

A large number of school libraries in the UK now have security systems installed. As the use of school libraries has grown and as the stock they hold – books, videos, slide collections, computer software – becomes more valuable, the justification for preventing theft is now very strongly based on cost. The cost of books and other materials has risen by about 250 per cent in the last ten years. The cost of security systems such as 3M (see Appendix 3), Knogo and Plescon has remained relatively stable. The advantages of security systems are that they prevent illegal borrowing or actual theft of library items. Many school librarians find that items will be taken unofficially by pupils and returned later. The items, however, are not always returned and in some schools theft is a large problem and school librarians may find that their limited budgets are stretched by the need to replace popular texts. Installing a security system may be funded centrally by the school and even the maintenance contract may not come from the school library's funds. Wilcox reports on the benefits of using the 3m system at Garth Hill Comprehensive where it was found that 25 per cent of the original stock in the school library had gone missing. The new library, formed out of the three original libraries, was an expensive addition to the school's resources and the cost of the security system could easily be justified.[2]

Security systems can also be justified on grounds other than cost. Bristol Grammar School's purchase of the Plescon system was justified on the grounds of cost but also on the grounds that pupils could now take bags into the library, thus making the library more attractive to users. Additionally, CDs, videos and computer software packages can now be displayed openly in the library whereas they were previously kept on closed access.

Choosing a system

The choice of an integrated system for a school library is an important one as the consequences of choosing a poor or inflexible system can be disastrous. The choice of system for many schools may be limited in that the decision on which system to purchase will be taken at LEA and not school level. There are many sound reasons for this, including factors such as cost, where the LEA may be able to negotiate substantial reductions for bulk buying for all schools within the LEA. Also, if all schools use one system, an authoritative database can be held centrally, as in Cambridgeshire, and schools acquiring the system can use this database to download records, thus saving much time and expense. Thirdly, as will be seen below in the case study, user groups can be formed locally and, as with the SIMS Library Management Module, nationally. This enables schools to be in close touch with the system vendors and also means that schools can put pressure on vendors to change and update parts of the system which are not user-friendly. Many schools in the UK do not have the support of a well-funded school library service and must make decisions in isolation. The following criteria for choosing a system should provide guidance for both school library services and individual schools wishing to automate their school libraries.

Criteria

(1) *Are the vendors an established company in the area of library systems?* Potential buyers should find out what products the company offers; whether they are part of a larger company; what the extent of the company's staff is; where the company is based; and, most

importantly, what the company's client base is. These factors are important in that the reliability of the system will be paramount and if the system has not been tested by a reasonably wide client base, there could be unforeseen problems in using it.

(2) *Can demonstrations of the systems be given?*
This may appear to be a very obvious point but it should be made clear to vendors that school library service personnel or teachers and school librarians will wish to see the system demonstrated not only by the salesperson but also by an actual user of the system in a school. Demonstrations by salespersons from companies are inevitably limited in that the demonstration usually uses a small database and searches are predetermined by the vendor. What cannot be seen from such demonstrations is how the system would cope with 18,000 entries as opposed to 180 or how easy the system is to use for the novice. Thus as well as having the system demonstrated at school library service HQ or in an individual school, buyers should ask the vendors to provide contacts with satisfied clients whom they can visit independently. Such visits will allow school librarians and teachers the opportunity to talk to their professional colleagues in another school about how effective the system is, to what extent the database is seen as a valuable educational tool, e.g. in relation to the use of keywords. In this way, an evaluation of the system working under normal circumstances can be made, problems can be identified and discussed and rational decisions can be made.

(3) *How effective is the system?*
There are a number of factors to be considered in relation to effectiveness. The layout of the system will be important. Instructions should be clear, and easy-to-follow menus should appear on uncluttered screens. The language used should be appropriate for use by the youngest pupils in the school. The system should be secure at all times so that, for example, when a pupil presses the Escape key, the system should respond, perhaps by flashing up an error message. The use of passwords should allow security of access to the database so that mischievous pupils cannot alter data. There should be, at all stages, a good Help facility on the screen so that if a user needs help s/he may press the F1 key, for example. Consistency of the Help facility is important and users should not be offered help at some stages and not at others and should be able to use the same key for help at all times.

Searching the database should be simple enough that even pupils straight from primary school should be able to use it with ease. In some systems, two levels of search are available:

(1) a simple search using one keyword and searching a number of fields;
(2) a more sophisticated search where pupils use a number of keywords which they can link using Boolean operators AND, OR and NOT.

Thus a pupil should be able to search for

FAMINE
FAMINE AND AFRICA
FAMINE AND AFRICA AND CHILDREN

It should not be assumed that only senior pupils or teachers will carry out searches using more than one keyword. In fact, given a school library stock of 20,000 items, pupils searching under only one keyword may well retrieve huge numbers of items, which will be of little help to them. Thus even Year 7 or Year 8 pupils may well prepare search strategies in the classroom and use these in the library to do relatively sophisticated searches.

A list of keywords used in the database should be available to pupils, preferably on screen. Some systems also encourage pupils to widen their searches by providing SEE and SEE ALSO facilities in the keyword lists. When pupils input keywords, the system should be flexible enough to cope with spelling errors. Right-hand truncation of terms should be available so that pupils can carry out initial searches on wider topics and then narrow their searches.

When pupils are carrying out searches, it should be easy for them to follow the instructions on the screen. Reading entries on the screen should be a straightforward task, with the pupil being able to evaluate the relevance of the items retrieved. Entries should have more than basic bibliographic information but should contain appropriate keywords and also, where possible, brief comments input by teachers on how the item might be used. Entries retrieved should appear on separate screens, in colour, and should be spaciously laid out. A pupil wishing to print out a search should be able to do this by choosing from a simple print menu.

In choosing a system, school librarians and teachers will be attempting to acquire a system which meets most of their needs. No system will be perfect and it will be a question of balancing the advantages and disadvantages of an individual system. As Lewins and Watson state: 'The advantages of flexibility and capacity in information retrieval programs frequently conflict with ease of use and simplicity in design appropriate for pupils.'[3]

Thus the fact that a system can handle the acquisition, circulation and cataloguing of 500,000 items will be irrelevant if its database is difficult to search. If the system is to be an educational and not an administrative tool, the needs of the pupils must be paramount.

(4) *What will it cost?*
The cost of individual systems will differ but the costs involved are not restricted to initial capital costs. School librarians and teachers will have to consider the ongoing costs of the system. There may be costs for initial training of staff. There will be a standard maintenance cost to be paid each year. Other costs include the provision of a printer and the continuing cost of paper and ribbons; and the purchase of new furniture or alteration of existing furniture to house the system. The cost of establishing the database, in terms of staff time, also needs to be considered and additional clerical help may be required for a time in the library to establish a fully keyworded database. As shown in Chapter 2, the justification for any costs in the development of library systems must be made on educational and not administrative grounds and support for the purchase of a system should come from both school librarian and teachers.

(5) *What support will be provided for the system?*
In choosing a system which is suitable for use in school, those involved will have to consider what support will be provided by the vendor. Firstly, there has to be agreement on the acceptance of the system. Thus the vendor, who may be supplying both hardware and software, should be asked to ensure that the system is fully operational and can cope adequately with a database of thousands of records as opposed to a few hundred in a trial period. Secondly, the exact nature of support – in terms of staff training and in the case of a breakdown of the system – has to be agreed. Thirdly, response times to problems are extremely important and buyers should ask vendors how quickly problems can be dealt with. For example, does the company have staff within a reasonable distance of the school or will the school have to wait a number of days before help arrives? The advice of a school or LEA administrator should be taken with regard to the above, so that a proper contract can be drawn up and guarantees ensured.

(6) *What plans are there to develop the system?*
While there is never a truly right moment to buy a computer system, school librarians and teachers should ask vendors what plans they have to improve their systems. It may be that a new, more powerful version is about to be launched and that the school should wait for the new version. The existence of user groups for the various systems provides a useful contact for independent advice about the development of systems. Questions about how system upgrades are managed and the likely cost of new versions of the software

should be asked before initial purchase. One particularly relevant aspect is the issue of networking, and the existence of networks in a particular school may influence the choice of system available. If the present version of a system is not networkable, vendors should be asked about future plans in this area. Compatibility of systems is not as great a problem as it once was but schools should be careful of buying systems which are not compatible with existing school networks as the cost of making the system compatible could be quite high. Advice from school or LEA experts in this area should be sought before a purchase is made. Schools should expect systems to be continually developed, especially in response to requests from user groups but should also try to budget for upgraded versions, which will not come free.

The above list of criteria is not exhaustive but covers the main pitfalls faced by purchasers of systems. Perhaps the key lesson for school librarians and teachers is to take advice from experts and existing system users before committing the school to purchase.

Case Study: Cheshire
Having consulted with other LEAs and having seen demonstrations of systems such as SIMS at other LEA schools, Cheshire decided to adopt the Heritage system as its integrated school library package. The decision to adopt Heritage was influenced by the favourable reaction of school librarians to the package; the support available for the system from Logical Choice; the firm's reputation in the field; and a favourable financial agreement which ensured that bulk purchase of the system would mean considerable savings for the LEA.

The Heritage system, a by-product of the Bookshelf system, is a standard integrated library system covering cataloguing, circulation and acquisitions. These three aspects are integrated so that bibliographic information is entered only once. Heritage operates on any PC AT 386 or 486. In terms of hard disk storage, Heritage advise that 1,000 titles will take up 1MB of hard disk space. The system will produce reports which can be integrated into word-processing and spreadsheet software and can be networked. Full security is maintained within the system which allows four levels of privilege to protect the main system functions.

The catalogue module has been the main focus of development in Cheshire. The automated catalogue is produced by entering details of records on screen (Figure 3.1) or by importing details from Bookbank or BNB on CD-ROM. A separate screen allows the input of keywords. The catalogue module has two levels of enquiry. The first is the 'Easy search program' which allows users to search using simple options. Searches can be made by author, title, keywords or on any field. Users can also establish the correct spelling of a word by using the index within the program. The 'Advanced search program' is for users more familiar with the system. The user can search using Boolean operators and carry out very detailed searches. The results of searches can be displayed in various ways and printing the results of a search is simple.

Catalogue Records

Bookshelf pc **CATALOGUE MAINTENANCE**

1) Standard No._____ 2) GMD _____ 3) Class _____

4) Title   1 _____

2 _____

5) Author   1_____ 6)_____

2_____   _____

7) Corp.   1 _____

Author   2 _____

8) Edition   _____ 9) Editor 1_____

2 _____

10) Place   11) Publisher

_____   _____

12) Year _____ 13) Accession   Location Status Due Date

1. . . . .

No. copies . . .   2. . . . .

Please enter a standard number (an ISBN or other, if prefixed by a letter)

Fig. 3.1

Heritage also has acquisitions and circulation modules. The acquisitions module allows ordering procedures to be automated and full integration with the catalogue module means that most catalogue details can be entered when an item is ordered. Order letters can be generated; items on order searched for and claims for outstanding items can be produced. The system has a budgeting facility which holds details of suppliers, and different budget headings can be catered for.

The circulation module holds a database of library users and can manage the issue, return, reservation and recall of all items. Traps can be placed on items or users. Overdue or reservation letters can be produced. A large number of statistical reports relating to the borrowing of specific types of stock (e.g. videos or books by an author), or borrowing profiles of groups of users (e.g. Year 10 boys), can be produced.

One of the key reasons for the successful implementation of the Heritage system in Cheshire has been the close links maintained between the Education Library Service and the Education Computing Service which produced a manual for the Heritage system designed specifically for use by school librarians and teachers in Cheshire schools. This harnessing of computer expertise has been invaluable in the progress made with the system in schools. Where technical problems have arisen, the Computing Service contact has either been able to solve the problems or has been able to contact the vendors in order to gain a solution.

The manual acts as a guide for school librarians operating the system but is used initially during INSET sessions during which schools are visited by a librarian from the Education Library Service and the Computing Service representative. Although the manual has to be technical in form, it contains many additional notes for school librarians which can clear up ambiguities in the manual produced by the vendors. A recent supplement to the manual (Figure 3.2 shows an extract) indicates the results of negotiations with the vendors on changes which should be made to make the system more suitable for use in schools. Once the system is established, the need for the manual decreases and more experienced school librarians will deal mainly with the supplements to fine-tune the system. Where there is a change of personnel in a school library, the manual provides an excellent base for the newcomer in her/his use of the system.

HERITAGE PC MANUAL SUPPLEMENT

Purpose
The following potential problems and relevant experiences in the application of Heritage have been recommended by members of the Heritage User Group. A cooperative effort is being made to highlight and overcome such difficulties: from expertise within the group or by reference to Logical Choice.

These notes will be collated as a supplement to the manual and will be updated as new problems/solutions are found. Recommendations given result from a consensus by members of the group.

The supplement follows the structure of the manual.

General
It is recommended that a record is kept of all cataloguing decisions, e.g. name forms. It is particularly important to record decisions about keywords used and to maintain an authority file.

1.4 DEMO library
It is recommended that DEMO library should *not* be attached, as machines have crashed at the attempted installation. Logical Choice will be asked to consider the removal of the demonstration from the software.

1.8 1.9 Entry of passwords
Before entry of passwords ensure that only one key press of *Enter* has occurred following date and time prompts.

4.3 Indexing
It is recommended that the index should be updated every c.50 entries. To update index select option *5 Update Index* from the Catalogue menu.

Fig. 3.2

The establishment of the database at The Ruskin School provides a typical example of the procedures for and the benefits of producing an online catalogue for the school library. As will be seen below, the benefits are seen not only by school librarians but also by teachers and pupils.

In planning the database at The Ruskin School, it was recognized that to produce an online catalogue which would be fully integrated into the curriculum, the creation of the database had to be a joint effort between teachers and the school librarian. The database is a reflection of the school curriculum and its planning and subsequent use had to emerge from the actual curriculum and not from ideas held about the school curriculum by the school librarian. The involvement of teachers at all stages was, therefore, vital.

In addition to help provided by the Education Library Service and the Education Computing Service, The Ruskin School librarian and teachers used *Keywords and learning*,[4] based on the MISLIP research, as the basis for creating the database. *Keywords and learning* proved popular with teachers as they recognized the potential links with information skills in the classroom and in the library and could relate the need for careful planning of the database to the teaching of their individual subjects.

The first step was to produce a questionnaire for teachers (Figure 3.3) which asked teachers to identify keywords for parts of the curriculum which they covered. It is a major task for any school librarian and individual teacher to discuss the identification of keywords for a *whole* curriculum, e.g. Geography Year 9, but the keywords for the database can be added in stages and there should not be an expectation that a fully keyworded online catalogue covering the whole school curriculum can be produced in a short time. By involving teachers at the stage of database *planning* ensures that when the database is created, teachers will still feel committed to involving themselves in further stages of keywording. The questionnaire also covered aspects of the use of materials both in the classroom as well as in the library and teachers commented favourably on the inclusion of class-based resources in the database as it clearly linked library and class-based resources in the eyes of the pupils.

The Ruskin School

Database planning questionnaire

Section 1 – Identifying keywords
1. What is the general topic/subject area you need to cover?

2. What related topics/ideas have been covered in class as an introduction or background to the topic?

3. List any words or phrases which have been stressed or defined as part of the background to the topic

1.	9. . . . .
2.	10. . . . .
3.	11. . . . .
4.	12. . . . .
5.	13. . . . .
6.	14. . . . .
7.	15. . . . .
8.	16. . . . .

4. Can you suggest any other keywords which you might expect pupils to think of in their first searches for information?

(cont.)

1. .... 4. ....
2. .... 5. ....
3. .... 6. ....

5. Which new ideas/concepts do you expect some or all pupils to cover in their assignments?
(Please includo any specific examples you would expect pupils to explore.)

Fig. 3.3

Teachers were also given guidelines for producing keywords (Figure 3.4) and, following discussions between the school librarian and department heads, lists of suggested keywords which teachers might add to were produced.

Keyword guidelines

1. Syntax
a. Singular for CONCEPTS e.g. sound, shape, communication.
b. Plural for NOUNS e.g. rivers, robots, insects.

2. Forms of names
a. Surnames, initials e.g. Hitler, A.
b. King Arthur, Mother Teresa, Napoleon, Leonarda da Vinci, Shakespeare.

3. Abbreviations
a. ATL – Attainment Level
b. NATL – New Attainment Level
c. WW – World War

4. Miscellaneous
a. Space – non fiction
   Sci-Fi – fiction
b. Drama – books about plays
   Plays – actual plays
c. Teacher resource
d. Folk tales, fairy tales

Fig. 3.4

The next stage involved the creation of the database. This is a very time-consuming task and help was forthcoming in the form of voluntary work done by one of the governors of the school. An important lesson here is that it is essential to establish clear procedures for new stock during the creation of the database. Existing stock details can be input reasonably quickly and keywords added gradually but once teachers were accustomed to using sheets based on input record sheets (Figure 3.5), they saw the value not only of them seeing the new resources before they went on to the library shelves but also the continuing value of each new resource being keyworded by a teacher or teachers. The new resources are thus seen by teachers as true curricular resources and not merely adjuncts to the curriculum which are housed in the school library.

The Ruskin School

Input record

1.	ISBN	. . . .			
2.	GMD	. . . .			
3.	Class	. . . .			
4.	Title	. . . .			
		. . . .			
5.	Author(s) Forename	. . . .	6.	Surname	. . . .
		. . . .			. . . .
11.	Publisher	. . . .			
12.	Year	. . . .			
16.	Series	. . . .			
17.	No.	. . . .			
19.	*Keywords*				
	1.	. . . .	9.	. . . .	
	2.	. . . .	10.	. . . .	
	3.	. . . .	11.	. . . .	
	4.	. . . .	12.	. . . .	
	5.	. . . .	13.	. . . .	
	6.	. . . .	14.	. . . .	
	7.	. . . .	15.	. . . .	
	8.	. . . .	16.	. . . .	
	25. Price	. . . .			

1.	Accession No	. . . .
2.	Location	. . . .
3.	Status	. . . .

Fig. 3.5

An INSET day was devoted to the new system at The Ruskin School. Teachers were given an introduction to the system and a county-wide picture of its use by the County Library Coordinator. The school governor outlined some of the trialling of the system done with Year 7 and 8 pupils. Staff were then given relevant books and input record sheets and asked to fill in title and curriculum-based keywords. One particularly valuable outcome of this was that teachers in departments could discuss the *relevance* of keywords with each other; teachers also commented that the keywording exercise in itself was a valuable tool for teachers to use in discussing aspects of the curriculum. Once the sheets were filled in, the details were input to the database. This allowed teachers to view the whole process, as searches could then be made using the keywords identified. One positive result of the immediate searches done was that teachers found that they retrieved a number of items as well as the book they keyworded. In many cases, cross-curricular resources were identified.

Searching The Ruskin School database has not proved problematic for teachers or pupils, and relatively sophisticated searches can be done by younger pupils. The method used to search on Heritage is fairly standard and HELP facilities appear at each stage. Figure 3.6 shows a typical search and some of the items retrieved.

		Catalogue enquiry	Date
No.	Hits	Search command	
1.	70	S* PLAYS	
2.	389	S* HUMOUR	
3.	15	S* 1 & 2	

No.	Author(s)	Title	Class
1.	Gray, N.	An earwig in the ear	822 GRA
2.	Walke, D.	Package holiday	822 WIL
3.	Townsend, J.	Taking the plunge	822 TOW
4.	Walker, D.	The bungle gang strikes again	822 WAL
15.	Arbuthnot, M.H. Root, S.L.	Time for poetry	821 ARB

Page 1   Q(uit) = [RETURN] OR S(elect)

Fig. 3.6

The advantages of having an integrated library catalogue at The Ruskin School have been reflected in all the Cheshire schools which now have the Heritage system. The main benefit lies in closer contacts between teachers and the school librarian and thus between the librarian and the curriculum. The use of the database now features in curriculum planning by teachers, and the school librarian is now more involved with teachers at the planning stage of the curriculum and not just at the implementation stage. The existence of the database has also raised the status of the school librarian in the schools involved. Librarians are now seen as more involved in the curriculum and also as technologically up-to-date staff whose expertise may be called upon by other school staff. The main benefits identified by teachers in The Ruskin School have included a clearer recognition of the place of the library in the school curriculum. Involvement in keywording has focused attention on not only the ordering of resources but their curricular use. Teachers also now more clearly see what the role of the school librarian can be in helping to plan and implement the curriculum. Teachers saw benefits in linking information skills teaching and the use of the database in that pupils were forced to plan assignments more clearly and think about the use of keywords not only in searching for information but in note-taking and in writing up work.

A further advantage to school librarians in Cheshire has been the existence of the Heritage User Group. This has allowed school librarians to meet to discuss developments in the Heritage system and to identify problem areas. For example, it was found that keywords containing two elements, e.g. NEW ZEALAND, caused problems as the system searched only under NEW and produced cumbersome results. The vendors were subsequently asked to address this problem in the software. The User Group also provides a useful context for new school librarians to learn from their more experienced colleagues.

The User Group has further advantages. The problem of professional isolation is a common one for school librarians who are often the only member of their profession within a school. By attending User Group meetings, school librarians can discuss common problems with professional colleagues and also swap ideas and experiences with colleagues. Thus the User Group serves as a kind of unofficial INSET for school librarians. The group meetings also allow librarians to report back examples of good practice from other schools to their teaching colleagues, who may in turn contact teachers in other schools.

Conclusion

The experience of Cheshire librarians and teachers with integrated library systems has been, on the whole, a positive one. There do exist problems with some aspects of the Heritage system, and the problems of finding time for keywording meetings between school librarians and teachers remains. However, there has been a change in many schools which has seen the creation of an online school library catalogue become the focus for more effective use of learning resources by teachers and pupils; improved curriculum planning; more attention being paid to the teaching and learning of information skills; and improved status for school librarians. The integrated database has acted as a valuable catalyst to produce improvement in schools in a number of areas.

References

1 Leeves, J. and Manson, A., *Guide to library systems for schools*, PCL, 1989.
2 Donnelly, J. (ed.), *The school management handbook*, Kogan Page, 1992, 191–4.
3 Lewins, H. and Watson, L., 'Classified information', *Educational computing and technology*, **11** (7), Nov. 1990, 13.
4 Williams, D. A. and Herring, J. E., *Keywords and learning*, RGIT, 1986.

4 The management of databases in the school library

Dorothy Williams and Anne Johnston

Introduction

The use of databases has been the focus for much of the early introduction of microcomputers in school libraries. Databases in this context are collections of bibliographic and/or factual information held in one or more files on a computer disk, and designed to allow the user to search flexibly and quickly for specific information within the file. As well as the many ventures into using small local databases, often developed on BBC microcomputers, the wide range of online sources already available to schools[1] and the advent of CD-ROM are enhancing the opportunities for the use of databases and other reference materials. We are already seeing the evidence of the interest and commitment to expanding the use of information technology with regional initiatives such as that in Lothian to provide CD-ROM facilities in all school libraries. The growing provision of commercial software specifically designed to enhance the management of school libraries is a sure sign that the application of information technology is expected to continue and that libraries will have increased access to a more powerful and flexible range of hardware than at present. The introduction of more powerful microcomputers such as the Apple Mac and IBM Compatibles, brings with it the possibilities of greater versatility from the library's point of view, while the user-friendly facilities of Apple Mac are encouraging more teachers and librarians. (The term 'librarian' is used here for a professionally qualified librarian or a teacher-librarian who manages a library to expand their own skill horizons.) At this important point in the development of the use of information technology in the school library, librarians and teachers must work together to ensure that learners gain maximum benefit from curriculum developments which stress the importance of information skills, and from the improvements in hardware and software. Librarians are faced with choosing from an ever-increasing selection of computer packages offering potential not just to extend the availability of databases but also the facilities for word processing, spreadsheets, graphics, etc. With limited resources (financial and human), the need for effective and efficient use of these resources is a priority.

Strong arguments can be made for the educational value of providing access to a wide range of databases in support of the curriculum. The ability to find and use information is central to the aims of developing effective and independent learning skills seen in Standard Grade, GCSE and 5–14. The introduction of databases in the school library not only widens access to information and to new media, it also has the potential to develop learning skills. One advantage of the computer over manual forms of information retrieval is that the user has greater freedom to structure searches to suit individual needs. By keying in one or more search terms e.g. subject keywords, author or title, the user can broaden or narrow a search without any predesigned classification structure. This places emphasis on thinking about purpose and structuring searches to meet information needs, an emphasis which can be beneficial in selecting and rejecting information at the later stages of reading, note-making and organizing information (see Figure 4.1).

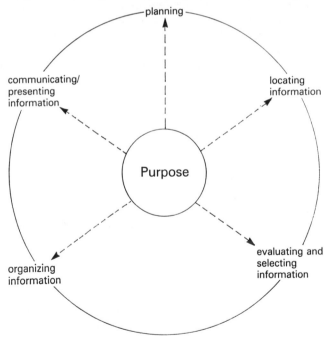

Fig. 4.1 The information cycle

The case for providing databases as cross-curricular resources within the library is, therefore, strong but alongside the opportunities which technology potentially offers comes the need to find the time to develop and exploit new tools such as databases. This will require careful planning and prioritizing - education generally offers little comfort to those seeking guidance on the way forward. Conlon and Cope[2] present a picture of *ad hoc* and haphazard change over the first ten years of the use of computers in education, highlighting a lack of long-term planning, debate and coherence in the use of such capital-intensive resources. There are lessons to be learned here for those who are currently making decisions about the future use of technology. These include the librarians and teachers seeking to take advantage of the potential which technology offers for expanding the information and skills base of learners. The key questions relate not to the technology as such but to the management of technological change within the school and, more specifically, in the school library. How then can we manage the introduction of databases to make it meaningful? How can we maximize the use of time and technological resources by building on what has gone before? What lessons are there for those planning change and for those experiencing it? The aim of this chapter is to identify some of the lessons which can be learned from the practical experience of one school, Dunbar Grammar School, which has been experimenting and developing the use of databases as learning tools for a number of years. It is not suggested that Dunbar can or should form a model for any other school. Each school and each school library must, to some extent, make its own decisions about the direction and pace which best suits its needs, resources and educational philosophy. By analysing one example, however, it is possible to begin to understand the local factors which are likely to influence the success or failure of technological initiatives. While the examples used will be from Dunbar Grammar School it should be noted that many of the issues which have arisen at Dunbar can also be traced in other schools which participated in the Microcomputer in the School Library Project (MISLIP) during the 1980s.

The Dunbar experience

A starting point
Dunbar Grammar School is a six-year secondary school of 543 pupils in a small coastal town in East Lothian, Scotland. The school library is staffed by one chartered librarian. In 1985 the school elected to take part in the Microcomputer in the School Library Project

(MISLIP), a Scottish Council for Educational Technology (SCET)-funded project based at Robert Gordon's Institute of Technology involving schools across Scotland. At this time the library stock of approximately 5,000 items was mainly book-based, with some periodicals. While the librarian was interested and keen to develop new approaches to information handling, she was faced with the usual dilemma of seeing a number of possible avenues but not knowing which to choose. The library has since gone from the situation of having to make a case for one computer to having an information technology area in the library housing seven computers with screen and printer output. Uses include in-house databases, CD-ROM and laser disk reference sources, word processing, spread-sheets, graphics packages, communications (e-mail, Prestel) and, most recently, the introduction of desktop publishing (DTP) facilities.

This, however, is only one aspect of the changes in information handling which have taken place in the library and classrooms over a seven-year period. The original library skills programme for S1 and S2 has developed into an integrated introduction to the library and its resources, including the concept of a database, in preparation for the later use of these tools. The information skills programme is currently under review as the school has begun work on a whole-school approach to information and study skills. While it is impossible to identify all the many influences at work on the school which may have had an impact, it is possible to trace the major factors which have contributed to the developments from the library perspective. Many of these factors have as much to do with people as with technology.

What have been the key developments which have stimulated this growth? What lessons have been learned at Dunbar? What are the long-term implications for further development? Before tracing the answers to these questions it is important to understand a little of what MISLIP was about.

The Microcomputer in the School Library Project (MISLIP)

MISLIP was funded by the Scottish Office Education Department (SOED) and SCET from 1983 to 1987. In summary the project set out to investigate the impact of a 'keyword approach to learning' on the development of information skills. The concept behind the project was that success in finding and using information was dependent on the learner's ability to draw on her/his own knowledge and understanding of a topic and a task. Real enquiry starts when the learner is able to use her/his own knowledge, expressed in the language of the curriculum and the learner's experience, as a starting-point in finding, evaluating and synthesizing information. Independence in seeking will only develop where the learner understands the link between knowledge and information. The use of curriculum-based databases in MISLIP was an attempt to provide information retrieval tools which would facilitate that link.

The major emphasis was on developing ideas and tools to encourage pupils to think about the topic and task and, from their own questions, derive some useful search terms. This 'planning stage' (see Figure 4.1) could then form the basis not only for finding useful sources of information but also for organizing and thinking about the information they were finding. The microcomputer was used at the stage of 'locating information', with small specific databases being developed by librarians and teachers for use in curricular tasks ranging from open projects to more structured exercises. The databases were indexed using keywords identified by teachers, librarians and pupils to form a more natural link between the language of the learner and the information resources available, between the curriculum and the library.

From 1985 to 1987 librarians and teachers in seven secondary schools throughout Scotland were involved in selecting areas of the curriculum to work in, and taking up and adapting ideas and activities which had been developed and piloted in one school in an earlier phase of the project. In practice MISLIP was involved in more than 50 separate curricular activities, with all year groups from S1 to S6, in a wide range of subject areas. Thirty-four databases were developed and used, and keyword mapping and project planning ideas were integrated into specific activities.[3] At Dunbar Grammar School this included databases for learning support groups, offering simple keywording and questions as reading prompts (see Figure 4.2), databases for mainstream mixed-ability classes (see Figure 4.3), and exercises involving group brainstorming and identification of keywords for projects (see Figure 4.4).

Reactions of learners in the second phase of MISLIP reinforced the findings from earlier stages of the project, namely that computerized information retrieval has the potential to:

- motivate pupils and teachers – one teacher commented that this offered a 'more natural way to find information';
- provide a wide variety of learning tools – examples range from straightforward bibliographic or factual databases to those designed to direct the learner towards tasks and advice in utilizing resources;
- encourage pupils to make connections between the different facets of thinking, planning and finding the information they need.[4]

CAVE: A database on cavemen for S1 Learning Support

KEYWORD	Weapons
QUESTIONS	What did they make weapons from? How did they make weapons?
SHELF NUMBER	573.3
AUTHOR	K. Lowther
TITLE	Early Man
PAGE NUMBERS	Part 12
SLS	Y

KEYWORD	Family
QUESTIONS	What did the mother do? Who was the head of the family?
SHELF NUMBER	573.3
AUTHOR	K.Lowther
TITLE	Early Man
PAGE NUMBERS	Part 11
SLS	Y

Fig. 4.2

The WAR database

KEYWORDS	Evacuees, air raids, Blitz, barrage balloon, rationing, land army, V-bombs, Hitler
SHELF NUMBER	941.084
AUTHOR	Kelsall F.
TITLE	How we used to live 1936-1953.
PAGE NUMBERS	USE the CONTENTS LIST and the INDEX to help you.

KEYWORDS	Battle of Britain, Luftwaffe, Blitz, Hitler, Nazis, U-boats, V-bombs, RAF
SHELF NUMBER	940.54
AUTHOR	Harris N.
TITLE	Spotlight on the Second World War.
PAGE NUMBERS	The INDEX will give you the page numbers you need.

KEYWORDS	Radar, Blitz, air raids, U-boats, V-bombs
SHELF NUMBER	327.174
AUTHOR	Headicar
TITLE	The arms race.
PAGE NUMBERS	

Fig. 4.3

Weapons	Defence
Spitfires/Messerschmitts	Home Guard
Land mines	Barrage Balloons
Incendiary bombs/V-Bombs	Land Army
Mine Sweepers	Gas Masks
Heinkel Bomber	Radar
Schmeisser machinegun	Siren/Air raid shelter/
U-Boats	Geneva Convention

Armed Forces	Germans
Home Guard	Luftwaffe
Luftwaffe	Messerschmitts
Land Army	Incendiary bombs/V-Bombs
Observer Corps	Heinkel Bombers/Schmeisser/
	Nazis
	Hitler
	Third Reich
	U-Boats

Air Raids	Civilians
Blitz	Rationing
Blackout	Blackout
Siren/Air Raid Shelters/Warden	Evacuees
	Identity Cards
	Gas Marks
	POWs
	Call-up

Fig. 4.4 Project planning: the keyword approach
Keyword clusters generated by a class discussing ideas for
projects on life during WWII

From: Williams, D. A. and Herring, J. E., *Keywords and learning*, Aberdeen,
Robert Gordon's Institute of Technology, 1986.

However, feedback was also gathered on aspects of the planning
and management of this kind of approach. The kinds of
'management' questions which were of interest included:

- How widely applicable would the ideas be?
- How easily could the ideas be taken up and adapted to suit
  different needs?
- Who would be involved – i.e. librarians and/or teachers?
- What kind of roles would librarians and teachers play?

It is precisely because of this broader remit that it is possible to seek
some longer-term lessons from the schools involved.

At Dunbar many of the lessons which have been learned from the early experimentation with 'learning databases' have been concerned with the thinking and planning which underlies database development and information skills development. It is these lessons which have helped the school move forward in its use of technology by providing a base for joint teacher/librarian planning, for successful integration of a range of technological developments, and for the continued pursuit of a whole-school policy for information and study skills.

Lessons

The need for integration

Databases in the library may be seen simply as an addition to the catalogue, another library tool, but this is only part of the picture. While they obviously offer the potential for flexible, fast retrieval of information in a way which tends to be more motivating than many traditional catalogues, they should also be seen as learning tools. If databases are to prove effective as learning tools, the way in which the learner is introduced to the technology becomes a key factor. The computer must be integrated within a wider approach which emphasizes thinking and planning as much as information retrieval *per se*. The most important factor appears to be that the database is clearly linked to the curricular task.

For example, the WAR database, used by S2 classes at Dunbar studying life in World War II Britain, is introduced only after some considerable time has been spent brainstorming, identifying useful keywords from the group's knowledge of the topic, clustering keywords under broader headings, and using this as the focus for choice of project topics within the general theme of WWII (see Figure 4.4). In this way the stress is on making links between 'what we know' and 'what we would like to find out about' rather than placing undue emphasis on the database itself. The keywords are useful when pupils use the database to search for information sources but also lay the foundation of structuring and organizing the information they find from those sources. Pupils are then more likely to see the computer, and the keyword search facility, as a means to an end rather than an end in itself. They can be introduced to the computer when they see a need to find information for their project and not as a separate exercise.

This kind of introduction implies a need for close collaboration between classroom and library, not just at the planning and design stages but also at the implementation stages. In practice in Dunbar the more formal introductions which were planned in the earlier stages of MISLIP have given way to a much less formal approach, with small groups or individual learners being shown the basics of keyword searching when they are ready to use the information. This is as true of the newer CD-ROM facilities as it was of the original small-topic databases of MISLIP. Again this has implications for class management in the library.

One of the most successful ways of introducing the information retrieval system at Dunbar has been to encourage learners to help one another, working in pairs, provided this is carefully monitored and supported by the librarian and teacher. This reinforces the introduction given by the librarian, and at the same time pupils gain confidence in their own ability in a non-threatening environment. In addition, now that computers are used in many departments in the school and Computer Studies is taught to all pupils, learners are much more confident using the hardware and help each other even more, often with very little prompting from the teacher or librarian. The problems of overcoming some learners' fears of using the technology which existed at the start of MISLIP no longer exist.

Questioning is an important part of enquiry and learning, and this too has been the focus of project planning in Dunbar as a preliminary to searching for information (see Figure 4.5).

1. How would they find coluors?
2. Did they have shoos?
3. Did they have wood?
4. What happened if they were ill?
5. What would they use for the drawings?
6. Did they play any games?
7. How would they find food?
8. How would they brush their teeth?
9. Where did they get there clothes from?
10. How did they make there weapons?
11. What kind of places did they live in?
12. How did they light a fire?
13. How did they cook stuff?
14. How do they wash?
15. Where did they do the toliet?

Fig. 4.5 Questioning and project planning

Questions about cavemen generated by a pupil before searching for information in the library

The value of encouraging learners to identify the questions they want to answer in their information search, was clearly seen when different approaches to a project in S1 Science were evaluated. Over

three sessions, pupils used a small database containi
to information sources in the library on animal and
the first two occasions considerable time was spent
pupils to generate questions from which keywo
identified; on the third occasion, pupils went strai
prepared lists of keywords from which they selected topics for
enquiry. There was little difference in their technical ability to use
the database but clear differences were apparent when using the
information sources they had identified. The learners in the third
group did not select information from sources so readily as those
in the first two groups. They needed to be prompted to begin taking
notes. Use of the database had become a means of locating resources
only and, having found the resources, the pupils seemed unsure
as to what happened next. In other words, the database search had
become an exercise remote from any real information purpose.

This behaviour implies a need for very clear identification of the
aims and objectives of using databases and of the role of the library
within the curriculum. It also emphasizes the need for close
consultation between the librarian and the classroom teacher.

Database planning

The importance of planning cannot be overstated. Experience at
Dunbar emphasized the need for effective librarian/teacher
cooperation at all stages of developing and implementing a 'keyword
approach to learning'. When developing small databases, the joint
identification of keywords, the discussion of the way a topic was
approached, the depth of coverage, etc., proved useful not just in
helping prepare a useful database but also in creating much stronger
links between librarian and teachers.

The planning framework developed by librarians in MISLIP (see
Figure 4.6) is still in use at Dunbar for the development of small
in-house databases. The needs and abilities of the learners are central
to the key questions of:

- What is the general theme or topic? (Subject area, focus, purpose ...)
- Who is likely to use the information? (Ages, abilities, previous
  experience, classes or small groups ...)
- What kinds of questions will they ask? (Their prior knowledge
  of the topic, approaches and examples used in the classroom,
  examples from teacher's/librarian's observation of previous
  groups ...)

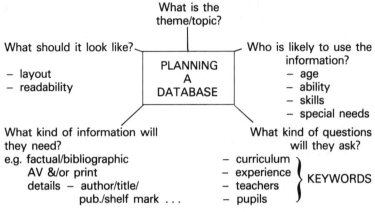

Fig. 4.6 Planning a database

From: Williams, D. A. and Herring, J. E., *Keywords and learning*, Aberdeen, Robert Gordon's Institute of Technology, 1986.

- What kind of information will they need? (Purpose of exercise, depth, coverage, factual information or references, range of media ...)
- What should the information look like? (Screen layout, detail ...)

Most database planning at Dunbar has been done through detailed discussion between the librarian and teachers, although these questions have also been used as the basis of planning pro formas in other schools (see Chapter 3). An invaluable addition to these planning stages is the development of small demonstration or trial databases by means of which the librarian and teacher can discuss the layout of the information on the screen, the readability of the screen, and the steps in keyword searching. For example, the CAVE database created for S1 Learning Support pupils at Dunbar, using KWIRS software, went through four different designs before the final version was agreed on by teacher and librarian (see Figure 4.7). Here the layout was critical to the readability of the screen but equally important was the need to include simple questions as reading prompts. The database has recently been transferred to another format using the FIND program (see Figure 4.2), an example of the way in which information technology developments continue to evolve as new programs become available to meet needs.

CAVE: a database of information about cavemen for S1 Learning
Support project

Early designs for the database using KWIRS software

1.

McCORD, A.   EARLY MAN.   573.3 S.L.S.   Beliefs   page 24 –
tools   pages 22 – 23 – weapons   pages 22 – 23 – fishing   page 23

TOPICS   BELIEFS
                TOOL
                WEAPONS
                FISHING

2.

HINDE, C.   THE FIRST MEN ON EARTH.   573.3 S.L.S.

QUESTION   WHAT
                DID
                THEY
                KILL
                WITH?

KEYWORD   HUNTING

3.

How did they make ornaments?   What did they make ornaments from?
LOWTHER, K.   EARLY MAN.   573.3 S.L.S.   PART 10

KEYWORDS   ORNAMENTS

4.

HOMES
How did they make their homes?   Where did they live?
MILLARD, A.   EARLY MAN.   PAGE 48

KEYWORDS   HOME
SHELF NUMBER   573.3 S.L.S.

(Format 4 was chosen and used successfully with several groups of pupils.)

Fig. 4.7   Developing a database

The questions being considered in the planning framework are, of
course, not confined to the production of databases. They would
be worthwhile questions in any situation where the library is to be
used as part of a specific curriculum task. As a result of this level
of information, the librarian has a much clearer picture of the

information needs of the curriculum generally, the approaches taken in the classroom, the ability and prior experience of the learners before coming to the library, and the adequacy of the library stock to cope. The framework has in fact played a much wider role in the planning of information developments in Dunbar. Database developments in MISLIP simply provided a practical demonstration of the potential value of this kind of joint planning for the evaluation of library resources generally and the stronger integration of library and curriculum. It provided a starting-point for the acceptance of greater involvement of the library at the planning stages of curriculum development, and for the library as an integral aspect of curriculum delivery.

Joint planning is also essential at the practical implementation stage of information technology. The integrated introduction of databases within curriculum can only take place if the practicalities of managing large numbers of pupils in the library are resolved. Classes using the library at Dunbar may find themselves sharing accommodation with seniors using the library for individual study and/or small groups or individuals from other classes carrying out research. In such a situation the careful monitoring and support, which is an essential aspect of helping pupils benefit from the technology, is only possible through cooperation between the class teachers and the librarian, and between different groups of pupils. At Dunbar the class teacher and the librarian work together to ensure that pupils can use the resources, as far as possible, at their own pace and that those who require individual assistance get it. Whilst the librarian introduces pupils to the computer database the class teacher assists pupils to locate resources on the shelves or vice versa.

Long-term planning
The integration of information technology within the curriculum is a time-consuming though important exercise. If one of the ultimate goals is to provide a worthwhile educational experience in a cost-effective way, the librarian cannot afford to indulge in an ad-hoc approach to the many opportunities for development which present themselves under the banner of initiatives such as TVEI, or new curriculum developments such as 5–14. There is a need not only to plan each separate development well, but to plan on a longer-term basis, working towards a meaningful pattern of development.

This might, for example, take the form of planning for a progression of increasingly challenging learning experiences across the curriculum. This kind of pattern can be seen in Dunbar where the aim is that information skills are reinforced by opportunities for pupils to use series of databases in different subject areas over a period of time. The databases are deliberately designed to extend the learner's skills by encouraging her/him to move on from databases which offer a small number of references with extra information (e.g. page numbers in references or questions as reading prompts) to those which provide a wider range of more basic bibliographic references, placing the onus on the searcher to utilize skills of using indexes, skimming and scanning, evaluating sources, etc. Thus Learning Support pupils at Dunbar gain great confidence in finding information in the library by using the CAVE database within their own group, before moving on to use the WAR database in S2 mainstream classes. The librarian and the Learning Support teacher are both in a position to be able to chart this kind of progression across the curriculum. Few others are in the same kind of day-to-day contact with teachers and pupils from different subject areas at different curriculum levels.

At Dunbar the librarian has found the Learning Support and the Computer Studies teachers to be vital contributors to long-term planning of information technology developments in the library. The Learning Support teachers can help identify cross-curricular needs whilst the Computer Studies teachers know the pupils' skills and abilities in using computers and also what developments are planned in information technology in their own department.

It is one thing to develop new information tools and new learning experiences; it is quite another thing to ensure that you are in the right place at the right time to recognize the opportunities and needs for such developments. While planning is crucial to information technology development, pressures on time mean that it is difficult for a librarian to take part in every curriculum planning meeting even if invited. It is even more difficult for a teacher with part-time responsibility for a library. At Dunbar the librarian has found it vital to get involved in consultation with teachers *between* meetings, to keep abreast of curriculum plans by ensuring she has adequate individual contact with principal teachers and senior management and, by such means, to ensure that the library has a voice in planning.

Nevertheless, some structured support from a representative group of teaching staff is needed to stabilize and embed developments meaningfully within the curriculum. While this is often the task of a library committee, more specific developments may provide a useful impetus. At Dunbar a TVEI initiative has resulted in a concerted move by a group of teachers and the librarian to analyse the information and study skills needs across the curriculum. A detailed questionnaire (see Figure 4.8) is currently being used to identify the kinds of skills which should be covered in S1, and this audit will eventually cover all year groups. The detailed picture which emerges will put all information skills developments on a firm footing and allow the librarian to evaluate and improve the present information skills programme, including the appropriate focus for information technology use.

STUDY SKILLS CHECKLIST Are pupils expected to be competent in this skill?	Is this important in your course?	Do you expect pupils to arrive in S1 with this skill?	Does your department actively teach this skill as part of course material?	If so please state which year group(s)
Can use an atlas				
Can use a bibliography to find further information				
Can use a telephone directory				
Can use almanacs				
Can use a thesaurus				
Can use non-book material (slides etc.)				
Can use Dewey numbers				
Can use a Card catalogue				
Can use Guide words				
Can use Databases				
Can use the Careers library				
Can understand abbreviations				
Section E – Organising information Can draw conclusions from given information				
Can make inferences from given information				
Can predict outcomes				
Can identify bias or unfairness				
Can differentiate between fact and opinion				

Fig. 4.8 Part of the questionnaire designed to audit information and study skills in the curriculum

© Lothian Region Department of Education, 1992

Long-term planning depends on clear identification of aims, objectives and long-term policy. Just as there is a need to find a realistic starting-point, there is also a need to develop a strategy for moving on. This will inevitably involve the librarian in seeking additional support to update or replace equipment, and to invest in additional hardware or software to ensure that the maximum opportunity for relevant hands-on experience can be provided when needed. A clear set of educational aims, such as those identified by the librarian in her submission for TVEI support for an information technology area (see Figure 4.9), has ensured that information technology development at Dunbar has progressed with a clear sense of direction.

Education targets
It is intended to achieve the following goals:
1. Make resources available to the maximum number of pupils.
2. Give pupils a chance to use technology to prepare them for technology in the workplace.
3. Promote equal opportunity for use of technology.
4. Promote student-centred learning.
5. Promote development of information-handling and investigation skills by pupils.
6. Develop existing Open Learning opportunities.
7. Improve availability of careers information.

Curricular areas and activities to be enhanced
It is intended that all areas of the curriculum will be enhanced by this development building on the work of S1 and S2 in using library resources, including databases.

Fig. 4.9 Excerpt from the submission for TVEI support prepared by the school librarian at Dunbar Grammar

Development depends on people
The development of any kind of integrated cross-curricular approach to information skills development remains dependent on the coordinating role which, in all the MISLIP schools, was played by the librarian. Changes in library staff tend to mean that further development of ideas is at least temporarily halted. This does not indicate any diminishing of enthusiasm on the part of the teachers involved but seems more likely to be a reflection of the need for a non-subject-based viewpoint. Without the stimulus of someone who has an overview of the curriculum, is able to offer suggestions and ideas from outside an individual subject base, and is able to work with the subject teacher in matching information needs with

curriculum aims and objectives, there is often a tailing-off of developments.

This has not been an issue at Dunbar where the librarian has been able to follow through developments continuously and, most importantly, to increase her own knowledge, skills and network of professional contacts to support these developments.

Experience at Dunbar has tended to indicate more clearly the impact of changes in *teaching* staff. While this can be beneficial, bringing with it new ideas, more computer literacy or different teaching methods, there can be problems for long-term integration of information technology and the library. A good example of this at Dunbar is the case of S2 project work in a department where two teachers were involved with the librarian in planning and developing worksheets and a database of resources to help support project planning and location of information. Joint evaluation led to further developments and progress, with databases and worksheets being updated and used successfully over a two- to three-year period. In other words there appeared to be not simply a development of a 'keyword approach', but also a development in the process of collaborative planning of information skills in the curriculum.

Subsequent changes in teaching staff, however, resulted in a continuation of the project within the curriculum but with no further consultation with the librarian. In fact new teachers appeared to have no knowledge of the previous collaboration or the availability of database and library support. While the project remains in the syllabus, there appears to have been little passing on of information about the existence of information systems and/or previous teachers' experiences in evaluating their own preparation and introduction to the project. This is being remedied by the librarian who has initiated discussions with the department concerned. The whole experience, however, indicates that an apparently well-integrated and jointly planned approach to information skills again relies for its continuation on individual staff, and on the need to monitor progress continuously. It may also call into question what we mean by 'successful integration' of information technology within the curriculum and suggest there is still some way to go in developing a curriculum-planning philosophy which includes the library and the information context as an integral aspect.

Roles and skills
As has been seen, the planning and coordinating role of the information specialist can be a crucial one. The introduction of information technology to a school library can have many

implications not only for time management and prioritizing of tasks, but also for the roles of the librarian. At Dunbar the introduction of databases and further development of information technology in the library has resulted in changes in emphasis and new roles as well as new pressures.

The successful application of information technology in the library has itself created a selling-point for the library, presenting a new image and awareness of what the library can offer. This has the effect of increasing the support for the library and offering new opportunities for development. Amongst the new roles the librarian has found herself playing has been that of helping to introduce teachers to information technology in a practical and non-threatening environment.

While all recent curriculum changes have created the need for more information skills, pressures on teachers' time can often mean that developments become problem-driven: new approaches are taken in response to problems rather than as interesting developments in their own right. This has in fact proved a useful starting-point for MISLIP developments in schools but does nothing to aid the development of a long-term strategy. In this the librarian needs to react to the immediate needs of teachers and pupils but must also be prepared to be proactive and to stimulate developments. This can include presenting new ideas and systems to individual teachers or leading INSET workshops, in keeping up to date with educational initiatives and identifying new information needs before they become apparent to teaching staff, or identifying opportunities for additional funding.

Opportunities and influences

While MISLIP provided a starting-point for information technology activities in the library at Dunbar it is only one example of the many influences at work in the school. Key *internal* factors which have created opportunities for the library have included the following:

- support of senior staff in promoting the use of the library as a whole-school resource and in developing the use of technology across the curriculum;
- commitment from interested staff in individual information technology initiatives and in long-term development of information skills (e.g. the Information and Study Skills audit has been initiated jointly by the librarian and a group of teaching staff);
- new staff bringing with them more skills in the use of technology and/or different teaching methods;

- the availability of staff development time to allow the librarian to promote the use of existing information technology resources.

On a wider scale, there have been many influences working from outside the school which have again offered support and opportunities:

- curriculum developments which place greater emphasis on information skills;
- TVEI, which has encouraged different learning and teaching approaches and provided money for enhancements in information technology;
- encouragement of student-centred and flexible learning at national level;
- regional decisions and support regarding technology (e.g. CD-ROM facilities in every school).

As a result of the climate and opportunities created by such factors, the librarian and teachers at Dunbar have developed their own ideas, skills and use of information technology. Some of the original databases developed as part of MISLIP are still in use, regularly updated to keep pace with the changing stock of the library. New databases continue to be developed where appropriate, but the use of computers in the library has expanded to include the use of CD-ROM, word-processing, spreadsheet, graphics and communications facilities.

Development will continue. The ongoing evaluation of the implications of 5–14 developments in Dunbar and local primary schools, and the skills audit being undertaken by the Information and Study Skills Group, will have implications for information technology support. The next step in the use of information technology in the library will emerge from careful evaluation of the stage Dunbar has reached in meeting current and future needs. While that next step will inevitably be constrained by the financial resources available, it will build on what is already there and it will be founded on an awareness of the educational potential of information technology in the library.

Conclusions

The experience of Dunbar illustrates the importance of people in the management of databases in the school library. In particular it emphasizes the importance of collaborative planning between librarians and teachers if progression of information technology developments is to be meaningful.

Finding a focus from which to explore information technology issues on a small scale can be a key to successful management of technological change. At Dunbar MISLIP prepared a way for maximizing benefit from developments such as CD-ROM and interactive video by ensuring that staff and pupils had already begun to accept technology in the library.

It is just as important, however, to move on from these early beginnings and to establish a sense of direction for the library. That direction must inevitably come from within the curriculum and within the philosophy of the school. If policies and aims can be clearly defined, librarians and teachers will be ready to respond constructively to the opportunities presented by information technology in the library.

References

1 Irving, A., *Wider horizons: online information sources in school*, British Library, 1990, (LIR Report 80).
2 Conlon, T. and Cope, P. (eds.), *Computing in Scottish education; the first decade and beyond*, Edinburgh University Press, 1989.
3 Williams, D. A. and Herring, J. E., *A keyword approach to learning*, Aberdeen, Robert Gordon's Institute of Technology, 1986.
4 Williams, D. A., Herring, J. E. and Bain, L., *The Microcomputer in the School Library Project. Phase 1 report*, Aberdeen, Robert Gordon's Institute of Technology, 1986.

e information services

Jan Condon

> Current curriculum objectives include the investigation of very topical issues, the development of information handling skills and the specific use of databases. Teachers should therefore be encouraged to explore datafiles online and, where they exist, CD equivalents, to become familiar with these resources. Teachers are urged to ensure that instruction and use are integrated with the use of other school and local resources rather than treated as additional or separate elements of the curriculum.[1]

The above quotation from Ann Irving provides an excellent context for discussing online information services in schools and the roles to be played by school librarians and teachers in exploiting this type of resource. This chapter aims to analyse the availability of online services and the cost implications of using such services; and the educational rationale for their curricular use. This is followed by a case study of the use of online information services in Solihull 6th Form College.

Online services and costs

Online services cover a vast range of electronic information and communication services widely used in academic and applied research, among the business community and to a lesser extent in schools. The services include individual databases, database hosts who offer a wide range of databases to the user, and services which include gateways to other databases and to electronic mail. Online services operate via a microcomputer through the telephone network to remote computers which store the data.

The best-known service to school education in the UK is Campus 2000 (originally an amalgam of Prestel and TTNS) but there are many others which range from the huge database hosts such as DataStar, DIALOG and FT Profile which encompass a large number of databases, to locally produced systems such as Dataview in the Midlands and Healthdata. Finding out what is available and suitable for schools in the first category is possible through lists published by National Council for Educational Technology (NCET)[2] or more generally published directories[3] and for the latter the School Libraries Group's publication *Freefax*[4] is an invaluable source.

To become involved with online information services, the school requires a dedicated phone-line, a microcomputer, a modem to convert signals to and from the telephone system to the microcomputer, appropriate software and a printer. All schools in the country were provided with a modem via a Department of Trade and Industry scheme. Local advisers will be able to discuss details of locally arranged initiatives related to online information services but if this information is not available, teachers and school librarians should contact NCET for advice. Online information services can be costly, depending on the extent of use and part of the school (or school library) budget needs to be allocated to this in advance of use.

Costs have always been the main inhibitor to the extensive use of online services in schools and even special offers for schools are still relatively expensive. There are in some cases, for example with Campus 2000, different levels of service available in the up-front payment, so there is an element of consumer choice. The more difficult element in costing is the cost of telephone charges and the charges made on some services for accessing particular types of information or for downloading or printing certain pages. The cost of staff time, including training provided for school staff, should also be taken into consideration.

The major databases have different charging policies which may include a single registration fee, line time, citations and information received and this may vary from host to host. Other services mostly based on local viewdata or bulletin boards are very cheap or free, apart from the cost of telephone calls and the user's time.

Why use online information services?
With the advent of CD-ROM, the advisability of using online information services may be called into question, especially as many online services now produce CD-ROM versions of their products. CD-ROMs should be seen as complementary to online services rather than as a stand-alone by-product of the services. The online service is the active, dynamic service, whereas the CD-ROM version takes the role of the archive. In some instances, CD-ROMs may only cover a specific period, e.g. one year of a newspaper, whereas an online search of a full-text database may allow the user to search for information over a longer period of time.

The potential curricular use of online information services is highlighted in the information technology guidelines,[5] an appendix to the National Curriculum technology document. In the examples provided for developing information technology capability in schools, the document outlines the desirability and importance of using online services. In History KS4, it is stated that 'Extra information is available from viewdata systems and datafiles, and from a fulltext database stored on computer (p.C23) while the information covering Modern Languages KS4 states that 'Pupils obtain pictures from a national database over a telephone line' (p.C21). The National Curriculum document also highlights the need for pupils to have access to the information-handling tools which are used in the business and commercial world, e.g. 'Pupils need to relate their own use of IT to its use in the outside world' (p.C14). As online services are widely used by business for financial, company and news information, providing pupils with an opportunity to use the same type of sources can greatly enhance the relevance of curricular topics for pupils.

Online information services are not used in isolation and their relevance to the curriculum will be enhanced where the results of online searches are used by pupils along with other information-handling and providing tools available in the school library. Teachers recognize that using online services can add to the need for that critical and comparative element required of information technology by the National Curriculum and can also help to raise, in a real working context, information issues such as data protection, bias, accuracy and confidentiality. Even the costs of online searching can be built into curricular topics and some teachers have built into business studies projects a costing element where pupils have to identify the cost to a fictitious company of obtaining business information.

The extent of use of online services in individual schools will depend on costs and local circumstances but also on how teachers and school librarians view the role of the library in the school. The more the curriculum becomes prescribed in the UK, the more unpredictable are the information needs of pupils and teachers. Thus in using online information services, the school librarian can demonstrate not only that skills identified in the National Curriculum are being encouraged but can also enhance the reputation of the library as an information provider. Some schools whose finances are limited have still been able to access online services by contacting local firms who have carried out searches for pupils doing projects or have arranged for demonstrations of online services for pupils in the offices of the company.

Online information services at Solihull 6th Form College

At Solihull 6th Form College, the online information service is now seen as an integrated part of the totality of services offered. Over the years, the service has gone through a number of changes from the early days of Prestel Club 403, where students were encouraged to investigate the value of the viewdata service for their curricular needs. The college was also involved in a British Library/MESU project which enabled students to carry out searches on commercial databases such as DataStar and FT Profile. The cost of searching these hosts was covered by the research project but since then the library has had to cover the costs of continuing to provide access. At present, the librarian carries out searches in consultation with students and teachers. Students now have access to CD-ROM sources in the library and this has helped to limit the amount of time needed in using online services and has cut costs. The use of online services can now be more easily targeted to the need for information – usually very up-to-date, dynamic information – and CD-ROM can be used for other types of information.

The management of the online service made available is an important part of the library service. Students are made aware of the availability of these services through course tutors, and demonstrations are provided where appropriate. Online services are also mentioned in publicity about information services to particular curricular areas, e.g. a leaflet about statistical services will cite Dataview as a source of census data.

The accessing of online services is often initiated by the library staff suggesting an online solution to an information problem. An enquiry form (Figure 5.1) is completed by a student or a teacher whose enquiry cannot be immediately answered or who has particular difficulties in finding the information needed.

A dialogue with the student or teacher (or both) follows. Keywords are identified and possible sources of information are suggested. If an online search is a possibility, another form is completed which will enable feedback to be recorded for future use. This activity is summarized in Figure 5.2.

Other important features of managing such a service include ensuring the confidentiality of the passwords which are used to access the different services; keeping accurate records for bill checking and charging other departments where appropriate or for analysis of use. Most systems allow for the analysis of use and cost to be consulted on screen and downloaded, but if several systems are in use in the library, it will be necessary to keep a running total of time/cost incurred.

INFORMATION REQUEST

	Date
Name	Tutor set
Course	
Enquiry	Keywords

Library use
ACTION   SFC Lib. checked

CONTACT

RESULT

Fig. 5.1

Activity	*Implications*
User requests help to find information	Discussion Assessment Check resource availability
Enquiry recorded	Keywords identified Online appropriate?
ITT form completed Request processed	Immediacy depends on staff available; telephone costs; when information is required by
Database selected Procedures and keyword checked	Check forms and manuals/guides
Search carried out	Librarian/enquirer
Result downloaded/printed out	Disk/copy filed ITT form completed
Search logged	Check against bills

Fig. 5.2

Earlier use of online information services at Solihull 6th Form College have been documented elsewhere.[6] The following sections reflect current use in four areas of the A-level curriculum.

Modern languages

The Modern Languages department was the focus of the work done in college in the British Library project. A change of syllabus meant that a large number of students were studying (in French) events in the current year in France. DataStar's French news agency service, ATSA, was extensively used, with some students proving themselves to be very competent searchers, acquiring the information needed in fairly short periods of time. Since the project ended, several changes have taken place and there is now more topic-based work in the syllabus and new teaching staff have arrived. In addition, the college now has to pay for its own online connection to DataStar. The database is still seen by teaching staff as an invaluable tool in gaining the up-to-date information which is required. For subjects like the advent of Edith Cresson, problems in the suburbs and the planning of Euro-Disney, ATSA provided information which was in French and was current. Figure 5.3 shows the result of a search on problems in the suburbs. The immediacy of the information obtained from the database is not the only important factor. The appropriateness of the language used and the length of reports which, as they are for use by the press, tend to sum up the main points of interest, were cited by teachers as important aspects of the use of ATSA.

Other uses of ATSA include information to help individual students prepare their topics for oral examinations and information used by teaching staff who have used parallel stories in English for French/English and English/French comprehension exercises.

AN 9106091707
DT 09 JUN 92 17.07
TI Malaises dans les banlieues françaises
   Nouvelle flambée de violence développement.
LD Paris 09 jun (ats afp) Des incidents mettant aux prises des groupes de jeunes, souvent d'origine immigrée, et la police ont de nouveau éclaté dans la nuit de samedi à dimanche dans les quartiers 'chauds' de banlieues françaises, où le chômage et la formation progressive de zones-ghettos entretiennent une fièvre quasi-permanente.
TX A Mantes-la-jolie (40,000 habitants, région parisienne), une groupe de 150 à 200 jeune gens, selon des sources officielles, a affronté la police durant une partie de la nuit. Grossissant au fur et à mesure de l'arrivée

(cont.)

de renforts, les jeunes, répartis par groupe de 30 à 40, très mobiles, parfois munis de cocktail Molotov, ont pillé des magasins et attaqué des véhicules. Trois policiers ont été légèrement blessés et six jeunes 'français d'origine maghrebien' ont été arrêtés, selon la préfecture. Une bijouterie, dont le rideau de fer a été defoncé a l'aide d'une voiture, a été pillée.

Fig. 5.3

Databases from Campus 2000 services have also been used, including TECLA for Spanish topics, with questions and vocabulary exercises appended to the information by teachers. In German, exercises on topical issues from Derbyshire's Feline services (now covered through BTS on Campus 2000) are used both for individual practice and in class. The German assistant has recorded some of the text to provide listening comprehension exercises.

Future plans for work with the Modern Languages department include a reconsideration of the databases used in the light of possible links with work experience and business-related language work, electronic mail links with French and German schools and the possible establishment of a Minitel terminal. Current access to Minitel is available to Edutel, the educational part of Minitel via Campus 2000, but further information on accessing the whole system can be obtained from France Telecom.

Geography
The Geography department wished to use the Birmingham Heartlands developments as a major case study for the 16–19 geography project A-level sets. Discussions took place between the department and the librarian on locating information about and contacts with the various partners in the projects.

Statistical information was required in some detail from the 1981 census on the areas being redeveloped, so that a socio-economic profile could be determined for comparison with the 1991 data as it became available. In addition, comparative data was needed so that students could make comparisons between an inner-city and a suburban area. Students study Nechells ward for a field day, including an environmental and residential survey, questionnaire and video. They also study St Alphege, the ward in which the college is situated. Different social and economic indicators are compared – for example, car ownership and unemployment levels show considerable contrasts – and students attempt to explain differences between wards while discussing the problems faced by the two wards.

The former West Midlands Joint Data Team produce and manage a viewdata service which provides this statistical data for the cost of a local telephone call. Dataview has enabled the library to gather data at ward level, download it and pass it on to the department which has been able to make use of it in producing relevant material which complements other resources and provides a stimulus for discussion. It is also made clear to students that they can have access to the database for their own individual project work if they wish to make comparisons with other local or national data. Figure 5.4 shows the result of a search done on Dataview on census information in relation to the two wards.

Nechells ward

	No	%
OCCUPATION		
Professional	740	6.8
Skilled non-manual	1440	13.2
Skilled manual	2760	25.3
Unskilled	4570	41.8
Armed forces, etc.	1250	11.4
EMPLOYMENT in		
Agriculture	10	.1
Energy & water	80	1.0
Manufacturing	3710	45.1
Construction	400	4.9
Distribution	1580	19.2
Transport	630	7.7
Other services	1710	20.8

St Alphege ward

	No	%
OCCUPATION		
Professional	2960	59.4
Skilled non-manual	1320	26.5
Skilled manual	260	5.2
Unskilled	300	6.0
Armed forces, etc.	100	2.0
EMPLOYMENT in		
Agriculture	20	.4
Energy & water	140	3.0
Manufacturing	1030	21.7
Construction	220	4.6
Distribution	960	20.3
Transport	110	2.3
Other services	2230	47.0

Fig. 5.4

Business studies and economics

These two subjects are obvious areas of the curriculum where information stored on online information services can not only be relevant but can also demonstrate a major use of information technology in business planning. Appropriate sources of information range from the Campus Prestel Business Information Service to Reuters Textline now available on FT Profile and DataStar.

At the College, there are three main areas where these sources are used extensively. First-year Business Studies students work on projects related to the Land Rover company. In order to provide students with relevant information, the library and the department work together to set up resources files on the company and on the motor industry in general. FT Profile and FT Abstracts on DataStar provide a quick way of updating the news with information found filed in the library. The students also use CD-ROM to search the previous year's information gained from newspapers.

For Economics students, the economic statistical service from the Midland Bank, available on Campus 2000, provides a brief sketch of the state of the economy in any given month. This is a particularly valuable source of information, in that the statistical service itself makes use of many other sources of information about which students may have read. Also, students can make month-by-month comparisons of the economy to identify economic trends. Without this kind of up-to-date information which is synthesised from disparate sources, students would have to rely on printed materials which are less useful in this context.

Other uses of online information in these areas have been concerned with individual enquiries from students. The Electronic Yellow Pages has been searched to survey T-shirt printers in a given area; Textline has been used to trace information about the fast-food industry; and DataStar has been searched to provide a profile of a prominent US businessman.

Theatre studies

The use of online information services is not restricted to particular parts of the curriculum and in Solihull 6th Form College the Theatre Studies course, which is a popular and demanding A-level course, involves students in carrying out a considerable amount of research as part of their course. Students work in groups or seek information for individual studies and performances. Discussions between the librarian and the course teachers resulted in the compilation of a resource box on *Measure for measure* consisting of information from the library and from teaching staff, including editions of the text, books on Shakespeare's theatre, illustrations of costumes and sets and reviews of productions. The reviews of different productions were seen as a highly important source of information for the students and further discussions took place to identify the different sources of information on reviews.

The result of these discussions was that a session was held with each group in the library. The session explored the printed sources available and then allowed students to carry out online searches of newspapers, with each group taking a different newspaper and contributing the downloaded findings on disk to the resource box. The students were delighted with this rich source of information and students now use both CD-ROM and online searching for individual research into plays and playwrights, asking for online searches when the CD-ROM searches fail to produce results. Figure 5.5 shows the result of a search for reviews of *Measure for measure* using FT Profile and searching *The Times*.

The Times
Issue 63,210

TMS 12 Nov 87 Arts (Theatre): Fallibility by designs – REVIEW of 'MEASURE FOR MEASURE' in STRATFORD (515)
by IRVING WARDLE
Nicholas Hytner's production opens with the thunderously amplified crash of a cell door; followed by the sight of the Duke (Roger Allan) trembling with dread as he signs the statute that will shortly put so many Viennese citizens behind bars.
At a stroke, the performance thus parts company from the long-prevailing idea of the absent Duke as an absentee divinity; a source of absolute justice in contrast to his fallible subjects.
By acknowledging that he is as fallible as everyone else, the production gains a coherence that leaves you wondering how MEASURE FOR MEASURE ever came to be labelled a problem play. Mark Thompson sets the first scene against the base of two gigantic
***PRESS RETURN TO CONTINUE,N FOR NEXT ARTICLE OR X TO EXIT
classical columns, which then revolve to display the festering stews of the city. A neat bit of scenic design also becomes a statement on the body politic: an architectural strip-tease recalling Lear's line on 'robes and furred gowns'.

Fig. 5.5

Online services as part of the total services
Online services play a significant role in Solihull 6th Form library's total information provision. They are not viewed as a one-stop solution to information needs but rather as both complementary services and back-up facilities. They have many strengths and can,

in some instances, be the only immediate solution to a student's or teacher's information problem. They can encourage and motivate users by giving them choice and control over what is taken from an obviously vast store of information. They can encourage more flexible working methods by providing extended resource facilities, including the possibilities of interactive communications with other schools and communities.

The attitude of the College's teachers and librarian has been to examine where online information services can contribute information, extend student capabilities in finding relevant information and add to their experience of using information in a more general information environment. One of the library's main aims is to reflect the best kinds of information provision found in industry and commerce – given financial limitations – thus raising student expectations of what they might find outside college.

The future of online services
With the increasing use of CD-ROM in schools, it might appear that the future for online services would be limited. However, as seen above, in some cases pupils and teachers in schools will require information which is so up to date that it is not covered by CD-ROM sources. The costs of online searches are less predictable than those of CD-ROM but schools should examine the *use* to be made of CD-ROMs before buying sources which may be little used. The same money might be better spent on gaining limited access to online services where the quality of information gained may be higher and may better reflect the actual needs of the user.

One possible stimulus to the greater use of online services in schools may come from the database hosts who have seen the great success of CD-ROM in schools and may be prepared to set the prices of online information retrieval at a level which schools can afford. Companies such as DIALOG and FT Profile have already made some headway in this respect and it is to be hoped that others will follow.

Conclusion
The use of online information services in schools is still restricted, partly by the lack of knowledge of what is available and partly by the costs involved. However, these services do allow pupils and teachers access to information on a global scale, can provide teachers with instant curriculum-related materials from news services and do extend the boundaries of school libraries. Taken together with CD-ROMs, online services can provide teachers and school librarians with new opportunities to widen the educational horizons of their

pupils and provide pupils with extensive sources of information, which, if used effectively, will enhance the learning skills of these pupils.

References

1 Irving, Ann, *Wider horizons: online information services in schools*, British Library, 1990.
2 *Online information services for schools: a select list*, NCET, 1990.
3 Hall, J. L., *Online bibliographic databases: a directory and sourcebook*, Aslib, 1986.
4 Akers, N., *Free fax*, SLG, 1989.
5 National Curriculum Council, *Technology in the National Curriculum: non-statutory guidance: information technology capability*, HMSO, 1990.
6 Condon, J., 'Present users into future users' in *Online information 88*, Learned Information, 1988.

6   Campus 2000

Angela Bell

Introduction

We frequently hear that we live in the 'information age'. As educators, whether working in the role of teacher or school librarian, we are acutely aware of the responsibility we carry in helping pupils to develop the range of skills they will require to function as independent learners.[1] Online information services, such as Campus 2000, offer pupils access to a wide range of information sources in support of the school curriculum. At the same time they can provide vital 'tools for learning'[2] in the development of research and study skills.

What is Campus 2000?

'Campus 2000: the Education Network' is a service to schools and colleges, operated by British Telecom and *The Times*. It offers users access to a wide range of online databases, together with the facility to communicate with other network subscribers anywhere in the world. Campus was formed in January 1989 with the amalgamation of two existing services, Prestel Education and The Times Network for Schools.

To access Campus, users require a microcomputer, suitable communications software (such as Campus Consultant or Dialup), a plug-in telephone socket and a modem. The modem (or modulator-demodulator, in full) converts the digital messages from the microcomputer into the analogue signals of the telephone system, and vice versa. It allows classroom microcomputers to communicate with mainframe 'host' computers throughout the world, for the cost of a local telephone call.

Subscriptions are available at two service levels, Campus Basic and Campus Plus, according to the needs of the user. The basic service offers electronic mail and computer-conferencing facilities, a directory of network users, LEA and Special Needs databases, together with a selection of databases on Prestel. The enhanced service Campus Plus provides users with access to all public pages on Prestel and a number of specialist databases. Subscription rates (as at March 1992) are given below:

Education subscriptions:
   Campus subscription £259
   Campus Plus subscription £359

Schools with fewer than 300 pupils
   (including *all primary* and *special needs*)
   Campus subscription £134
   Campus Plus subscription £184

The main features of Campus 2000 are online databases, electronic mail and computer-conferencing facilities. The system comprises two broad areas, 'Campus Prestel' and 'Campus Gold' (see Figure 6.1). The Prestel service is a videotext system offering users over 300,000 pages of constantly updated information, and available from anywhere in the UK for local call rates. Campus Gold may be accessed either directly via the British Telecom GNS Diaplus Network, or via a 'gateway' from Prestel. Gold provides powerful and sophisticated communications services, including electronic mail and conferencing, plus its own range of databases.

A number of premium services are also available through Campus 2000. These are database services offered by other information providers at specially negotiated rates. Premium services currently include NERIS (information on education resources) and ECCTIS (higher and further education database). Additional subscription charges are required to access these services.

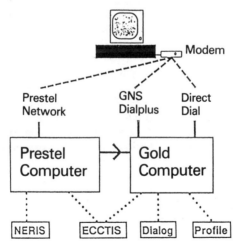

Fig. 6.1

Campus Prestel offers users a vast range of information relevant across all curriculum areas. The collection of databases includes news stories, weather and sports reports, TV schedules, a gazetteer of Britain, financial and business data and tourist information from around the world. The system also plays host to TECLA, a magazine section in Spanish. In addition Prestel provides users with a 'gateway' into other major databases such as Phonebase (all UK telephone numbers), Electronic Yellow Pages (a classified guide to businesses) and the British Rail database, all of which are available without any additional cost.

Prestel also features a selection of databases concerned specifically with pupils who have special educational needs. The SEND database is maintained by the Scottish Council for Educational Technology and special needs teachers throughout the country. It offers over 3,000 pages of up-to-date information relating to the use of new technology with special needs pupils. VIS (Visual Impairment Service) provides a wide range of information on education, welfare and leisure topics for partially sighted learners. VIS is designed to be used by pupils themselves, so all information is presented in double-height text.

CHATBACK is a magazine-style service developed and run by pupils with communication impairments. Designed to appeal to other students, CHATBACK includes a 'club corner' with features on hobbies, interests and writing activities. The database also includes a wide range of curriculum-related information of interest to all school pupils.

Information on Prestel databases is presented in 'viewdata' format and the frames, or pages, are linked together in a menu structure which is straightforward to search. An alphabetical index of both subjects and information providers is available online. More rapid searches can be carried out by typing in subject keywords. Alternatively, once a frame of useful information has been located, the searcher can make a note of the page number and can use this in a subsequent search to locate the information more directly.

Once a search on Prestel has been completed, individual frames may be printed out direct from the screen. Alternatively, frames can be saved and then downloaded onto the user's computer disk. This allows information to be viewed or printed out when the user is off-line, thus reducing telephone costs.

A large number of information providers (known as IPs) are represented on the Prestel system. They include both commercial and non-profit-making organizations. Many of these publish additional resources to support the curriculum. In these cases special 'response frames' may be available on the database. These interactive pages allow users to order items such as pamphlets direct from the information provider, simply by typing in the number of items required.

From Campus Prestel users may pass through a one-way gateway into the Campus Gold area of the service. The databases on Gold provide information on a wide range of curriculum-related topics. These include modern languages services such as Feline (French, German and Spanish news items) and Modlang; the National Environmental Database maintained by King's College, London; and careers databases such as the Electronic Job Book, online version of the Hobsons publication. Many local authorities, professional associations and other organizations maintain their own information services on Campus 2000. At national level, the INDES database features all press releases issued by the Department of Education and Science, together with the complete text of all circulars and documents issued for headteachers.

Unlike Prestel with its viewdata format incorporating colour and graphics, information in the Gold system appears in 'text' format. The screen output resembles the scrolling text of a word-processing package. Databases may be searched either by selecting items from a menu or by using keywords. Once a search has been carried out, the enquirer can scan the headlines of the retrieved material and then select which items s/he wishes to read. Keyword searches can be refined by combining search terms with the Boolean operators AND, OR and NOT to increase the relevance of the items retrieved. Wildcard symbols may be used at the beginning or end of search terms to retrieve items on related subjects. Once an item has been retrieved from the database, it can be downloaded onto disk for printing out off-line. The searcher may choose to edit the final format of the retrieved items by dumping the file into a word-processing or desktop publishing program, before finally printing it out.

Campus Gold also features a number of 'premium' databases which are available to all users for an additional per-minute connection charge. These services are managed by third-party information providers, with whom users will need to register before carrying out a search. For instance, by paying a connection charge of 25p per minute, schools have access to the Deluge Classmate service. This enables them to link up with DIALOG, one of the largest databanks in the world, based in Palo Alto, California. Campus 2000 users can search nearly 100 DIALOG databases which have been specially selected for their educational content. These include Facts on File, a full-text weekly news service covering publications from the USA, Canada and Britain; major US newspapers such as the *Boston Globe* and *Los Angeles Times*; and the

ICC British Company Directory. Information is held in four formats: full text, bibliographic records, directories of documents and numeric data. Searchers have the choice of using either menu mode, which offers a high level of online help and is therefore especially suitable for novices, or command-driven mode.

Command mode allows users to type in search terms direct, instead of having to work their way through a series of menu options. This results in more cost-effective information retrieval.

A further example of a premium service available on Campus Gold is 'Profile', which may be accessed at a rate of 60p per minute. Profile provides the full text of articles from the quality UK press and *New scientist*, over the last three years. Articles can be retrieved from the database by using free-text searching and downloaded to disk or printed out.

Other premium services may be accessed via Campus 2000 on payment of an additional annual subscription. These include ECCTIS (the UK courses information service), featuring data on opportunities in further and higher education. During the summer, ECCTIS carries a course-clearing service on Campus 2000, in conjunction with UCCA and PCAS. The database is updated daily with details of vacancies on full-time higher education courses.

Subscribers may also access the NERIS database. The National Educational Resources Information Service comprises around 40,000 items which may be searched by subject, age, phase or media. The database includes many ready-to-use educational resources, such as worksheets and magazine articles which are complete in themselves and may be downloaded onto disk.

Campus also provides users with access to a number of electronic 'noticeboards'. These are the online equivalent of a card in a shop window or on a school noticeboard. Noticeboards are available on Gold and also in several of the Prestel databases such as SEND, VIS and CHATBACK. Subscribers can read existing notices in a range of categories, or enter a notice of their own. This area of the system allows users the opportunity to request help with a specific project or to set up contacts with other schools on the network.

This ability to communicate with other network users is developed more fully in the electronic mail and computer-conferencing areas of Campus 2000. Electronic mail allows schools to send messages anywhere in the world, using the BT 'Telecom Gold' system, at local telephone call rates. Text can be prepared off-line in the classroom, using a standard word-processing package, and then uploaded into the electronic mail area of Campus Gold. Incoming mail can be read immediately, downloaded onto disk for subsequent editing, filed for future reference or printed out immediately.

Electronic mail enables users to maintain and develop links with neighbouring schools, local education officers or other network users anywhere in the world. Information on users is contained in ENQUIRE, a fully searchable online directory. Educational links can be set up and maintained between users with a far more rapid response than is possible with conventional communication methods. In addition, a number of interactive projects have been developed recently using electronic mail as the medium for communication. For instance, during the termly 'Newspaper Days' news reports are transmitted directly into the classroom and pupils are required to work collaboratively to publish their own newspaper, before the given deadline. The European Newspaper Day, organized by Cleveland LEA in 1991, required schools to produce a newspaper in a modern European language and featured authentic text items from France, Germany and Hispanic-speaking American schools.

Electronic mail is essentially a one-to-one method of communication. However, computer conferencing offers groups of users the opportunity to work together, under the guidance of a 'moderator' or organizer. The conferencing facility on Campus 2000 is known as 'Caucus' and is available to all subscribers, simply by selecting the conferencing option from the system main menu.

There is currently a wide range of online conferences available on Caucus. Many of the topics for discussion, such as 'Health' and 'Environment' directly support the curriculum. Others such as 'Newsline' invite both pupils and staff to discuss issues of topical interest. Some conferences are public, that is, open to all subscribers, while others are for closed user groups. To join a closed conference, users must first contact the conference moderator for permission to participate. In some cases, a closed conference may have been set up for a well-defined user group, such as staff training within an education authority.

Caucus conferencing operates in a similar way to a conventional committee meeting, except that discussion takes place independent of time and location. Users can therefore join a conference at a time and place to suit themselves. Caucus is currently being used for a variety of purposes: as a vehicle for delivering open- and distance-learning packages, as a method for collaborating on a particular project, such as co-authoring a publication; and for preparatory or follow-up work resulting from a physical meeting. Computer conferencing allows pupils to discuss a wide range of topical issues with other students from different cultural and geographical backgrounds, without needing to leave the classroom. The 'School Librarians' conference offers library staff a forum to share ideas and concerns with others working in the same area. It hopes to combat some of the isolation felt by professional librarians working in schools.

Each conference is made up of a number of discussion items, to which users are invited to make a response. The overall direction of the discussion is controlled by the moderator. A complete record of the discussion on any topic is available on screen and may be downloaded and printed out. Online conferences with a large number of discussion items may also be searched using keywords, in order to produce a list of items on a particular topic.

Campus 2000 provides subscribers with a comprehensive *User guide,*[3] outlining the facilities available on the system and including a number of tutorial exercises to develop users' expertise in each area of the service. The guide also includes a cost analysis of the telephone charges generated by using the system, ranging from 11.5p (cheap rate) to 43.8p (peak rate) for a typical ten-minute connection. A termly newsletter includes case studies and ideas for cross-curricular and collaborative projects. Other information is published in an 'Update' file on the system, the contents of which are highlighted to users each time they log on.

Case Study: Holywells High School
Holywells High School is a coeducational comprehensive school, with 830 pupils on roll aged between 11 and 16. The school serves a residential area of south Ipswich and includes an area special class for pupils with specific learning difficulties.

Holywells is a member of the Ipswich Initiative, a consortium of twelve secondary schools from both maintained and independent sectors within the borough. The Initiative aims to work as a partnership with local businesses and industry to increase the provision of computers within member schools and to provide training in information technology skills for teaching staff.

Campus 2000 is available in the school library, which is staffed during term times by a chartered librarian and a part-time clerical assistant. The library is equipped with two stand-alone RM Nimbus microcomputers. The room is not timetabled for teaching purposes. A booking system operates so that the library may be used for research by whole classes, small groups or individual pupils. The library is also available to pupils every lunch-time for individual research and to promote leisure-time reading.

The school has subscribed to the Campus Plus service since 1990 and funding for both subscription and online telephone costs is met from the information technology budget. The system is accessed via a Nimbus PC186 computer, using Dialup Educational communications software. Campus 2000 is used for information retrieval and research purposes, alongside a variety of traditional and electronic media. These include the Suffolk County Council online database SCILSdata which provides local information, and a range of databases to support the curriculum on either floppy disk or CD-ROM.

Both pupils and staff at Holywells use Prestel databases to access topical information which is relevant across the curriculum. Pupils are familiar with constructing and manipulating simple electronic databases, such as GRASS, from the information technology course taught in Years 7 and 8. Using databases in the library reinforces these experiences and provides students with the opportunity to develop a range of manipulative, cognitive and communication skills.[3] Traditional information skills such as formulating keywords, skimming and scanning text, and note-taking can be incorporated into the retrieval process. The use of online databases also reinforces the concept of the school library as part of a much wider network of information sources.

Pupils generally find the Prestel system simple to search and the information contained in it easy to read and understand. This is due to a combination of factors: the clear menu structure of the database, the use of on-screen colour and graphics and the level of online help provided by the system. Each frame contains a limited amount of information which pupils can assimilate before moving on to the next page. The communications software allows frames to be downloaded and saved for later viewing or printing when the user is off-line. This helps to reduce telephone costs and is particularly useful where several pupils need access to the same information at different times during the school day. Basic search procedures for use with Prestel databases are displayed next to the computer (see Figure 6.2) and the librarian is always on hand to oversee the search and provide guidance.

CAMPUS Special
Quick Guide to Prestel Routines

* Page number£	goes directly to a specific page
*£	goes back to the page before (NB you can only turn back a maximum of three pages)
**	deletes a mistakenly keyed input
*00	redisplays the page (NB use when 'line noise' or interference appears)
*90£	finishes your call to Prestel

Fig. 6.2

Databases on the Gold system, however, are less appropriate for pupils to search themselves, especially where students are younger or less able. The 'text' format is not as user-friendly as the viewdata screens of Prestel, with their greater level of on-screen help. The enquirer needs to possess more highly developed search skills and a greater understanding of how online information is structured and can be exploited. This is especially true of premium databases such as Profile and DIALOG which incur additional time charges. These two services are regularly used at Holywells to provide access to current news stories from a range of international newspapers and journals. The online services complement other newspaper databases held by the library, such as *The Times* and *Sunday Times* on CD-ROM.

Searches on Gold databases are carried out either by the school librarian or by the information technology coordinator. Enquirers are asked first to fill out a search request form, specifying the nature of the topic and helping staff to identify keywords and plan the search off-line. The forms also provide the library with a record of the department requesting the search, the time spent online and the telephone costs incurred.

Some examples of information retrieved from Campus 2000 are given below.

I need some up-to-date information on genetic engineering, especially in relation to diseases such as cystic fibrosis.

A science teacher was looking for journal articles to support a biotechnology unit for ten pupils. This topic had been heavily featured in the media and she particularly remembered a recent article from *New scientist*. Since the library at Holywells does not subscribe to this journal, the librarian and the teacher carried out a search on Profile and were able to retrieve the item, together with a number of other recent articles on related topics. These were printed out to create a topic file which was then passed on to other members of the department who were teaching the unit. The enquirer found the information valuable since it was highly topical and she felt it made the subject more relevant to her students.

Do you have any information to help me plan a holiday to France?

This request came from one of a group of pupils working on an 'open-ended task', or OET, as part of GCSE Maths coursework. Her task was to collect data enabling her to plan and cost a holiday to a destination of her choice. The pupil was first asked to identify her search terms. She then carried out a keyword search on Prestel, successfully retrieving several frames of tourist information. These frames were saved to disk and viewed off-line once the search was complete. The frames were retained (see Figure 6.3) and later made available to other pupils from the group who were researching similar topics. The OETs required pupils to demonstrate a range of practical data-handling skills, including collecting information from a range of relevant sources, judging whether data was directly comparable, and discriminating between necessary and redundant data.

FRENCH RAILWAYS	460452901a	0p
French Railways/TGV	071 491 1573	

Tariff Paris to main destinations of TGV Sud Est

	One Way		Return	
	1st	2nd	1st	2nd
	£	£	£	£
Albertville	45.30	30.20	90.60	60.40
Bourg St.Maurice	50.20	33.50	100.40	67.00
Dijon	26.10	17.40	52.20	34.80
Geneva	43.60	29.10	87.20	58.20
Grenoble	44.70	29.20	89.40	59.80
Lausanne	43.60	28.70	87.20	57.40
Lyon	37.60	25.10	75.20	50.20
Marseille	56.70	37.90	113.40	75.80
Montpellier	55.60	37.10	111.20	74.20
Nice	68.70	45.90	137.40	91.80
Nimes	52.80	35.30	108.60	70.60

Key __ Supplements   1 Main Timetable
2 Essential Info 0 Sud Est Index

Fig. 6.3

I need to write to several games manufacturers. Can you find me their addresses?

A class had been set the task of designing a travel game as part of their GCSE Craft, Design and Technology coursework. Several pupils decided to write to well-known manufacturers for advice on design aspects. The librarian chose one of the range of databases available through DIALOG Classmate. The ICC British Company Directory provided addresses of several companies working in this area.

Do you have any information on recycling nuclear waste?

Recycling is a topic which forms part of both the Science and Humanities curricula at Holywells, and a wide range of resources are available for research. However, there was a limited amount of information in the library on recycling nuclear waste. Pupils therefore decided to carry out a keyword search on Prestel using the search term 'energy'. They discovered that UK Nirex Ltd was one of the information providers on the database. Further information on this topic was available by completing an interactive response frame and the librarian was able to order additional materials direct from the company (see Figure 6.4).

GWV   53318351a   0p
UNITED KINGDOM NIREX LIMITED
ABOUT OUR COMPANY

UNITED KINGDOM NIREX LIMITED was formed by the British Nuclear Industry to plan and implement the safe management of radioactive wastes.

A private company, Nirex shareholders comprise British Nuclear Fuels plc, UKAEA and Scottish Nuclear Ltd.

HM Government, through the Secretary of State, holds a single special share and appoints two directors to the company's board.

KEY 1 TO CONTINUE   0 INDEX
9 TO ORDER FURTHER INFORMATION

GMV   53318359a   0p
United Kingdom Nirex Limited
TO REQUEST FURTHER INFORMATION

NAME
TYPE OF BUSINESS (IF APPL)

HOLYWELLS HIGH SCHOOL
LINDBERGH ROAD
IPSWICH
SUFFOLK
IP3 9PZ
0473 729222
Mbx 888229019

IF YOU WOULD LIKE FURTHER INFORMATION
KEY 1 IN SPACE PROVIDED

THANK YOU FOR YOUR INTEREST
Fig. 6.4

I'm writing an essay on whether boxing should be banned. Have you any background information?

This request came from one of a group of pupils researching current affairs topics as part of GCSE English coursework. Pupils are required to write a discursive essay on a controversial topic of their own choice, presenting a range of views and arguing their own case. Research is carried out in the library at the beginning of the assignment, using a variety of information sources. Since there was little information on the ethics of martial arts in printed form, an online search was performed on Profile and a number of recent newspaper articles were retrieved. These articles then formed the basis of a topic file which was available for staff to use in class.

Can you find me any recent articles on mixed-ability teaching?

Two possible sources of educational abstracts are available on Campus 2000: the FELINE TEASE database available on Campus Gold, and the American database ERIC, which may be accessed through the DIALOG Classmate premium service. The TEASE service, managed by Nottingham Polytechnic, offers keyword-searchable abstracts from nearly 100 education journals. A list of the journals included, and indexing terms used, had already been printed out and circulated to staff responsible for in-service training. A keyword search was carried out on TEASE and details of several articles were retrieved.

These examples can give little more than a 'taste' of the enormous range of topical information available on Campus 2000 and the cross-curricular opportunities for its use. As well as providing a tool for research and retrieval in the school library, Campus has been integrated into a number of curricular projects at Holywells.

'The Krypton Factor' was devised as part of an activity week for lower-school pupils, towards the end of the summer term. It involved over 300 students from Years 7 and 8. Pupils were assessed in a variety of skills areas and an important factor was their ability to work as part of a team.

An information-gathering task was included in the programme, requiring each group of pupils to produce a holiday brochure on a European country, within a strict time-limit. The activity was planned collaboratively by teachers, the IT coordinator and librarian so that a wide range of up-to-date information sources was available. Prestel was accessible throughout the activity, with each group receiving a timetabled 'slot' for gathering online information. Pupils were required to demonstrate a wide range of skills through this activity: selecting information sources, gathering data, evaluating its usefulness and accuracy, and synthesizing the information into its final form. The collaborative nature of the activity required pupils to display problem-solving skills and the ability to delegate tasks within the group.

Electronic mail and computer conferencing are used by staff at Holywells to communicate with other schools, both locally and internationally. A group of Year 9 English pupils were asked to write letters about everyday life in a typical English secondary school. The correspondence was prepared on a word processor, uploaded into the electronic mail system and sent to a secondary school in Japan. Replies were received from Japanese pupils who were studying English as a foreign language. E-mail enabled the pupils to communicate far more rapidly than would be possible with conventional mail and gave them the opportunity to write for an audience of their own age group, but from a different cultural background.

Computer conferencing allows staff to send messages to a group of users on the network. A Caucus conference has been created specifically for schools within the Ipswich Initiative. This is used as a forum for sharing good practice and as a practical method of organizing staff INSET. Since the moderator can check whether an item has been read by an individual user, this is an efficient method of publicizing forthcoming events. Library staff use conferences such as 'Health', managed by the English Nursing Board, as a means of gathering up-to-date information and resources on curriculum-related topics.

Teaching staff at Holywells welcome the wide range of topical information that online databases provide in a convenient and highly accessible form. Users have found the Prestel database particularly easy to search using keywords or the alphabetical index. Campus 2000 has helped to raise the profile of the library within the school and increased staff awareness of the wider information network. The online information service provided by the library has encouraged a number of subject departments, who had little previous contact with the library, to use it for research.

Campus 2000 is perceived by some staff as an expensive resource, due to its online costs, especially when compared with other database technologies such as CD-ROM. Campus has an important advantage over these media, in that its databases are updated far more rapidly. For instance, the Profile service on Campus Gold is updated with news stories on a daily basis: newspapers published on CD-ROM are issued quarterly and may be as much as three months out of date. Online services are ideally used to complement other databases, providing schools with access to a wider range of sources and the most up-to-date information available.

Careful management of the way Campus is used can significantly reduce online costs. For instance, a number of topics may be searched in a single session and the search carried out at an 'off-peak' charging period. When using premium services such as Profile, it is vital that the search strategy is thoroughly prepared before going online, to make the retrieval as rapid as possible. Familiarity with the structures of the various databases on Campus will inevitably result in more efficient searching. In many cases the experienced user can dispense with the on-screen prompts given in menu mode and type in search commands direct to retrieve material more rapidly. At the end of the search, materials can be downloaded from the databases, for later viewing, editing or printing out.

The employment of a qualified librarian to manage the system within the school ensures not only that online costs are controlled but also that the full range of databases is exploited to support the curriculum. Campus 2000 is a constantly developing system. In a rapidly changing education sector, teachers have many other demands on their time. The professional librarian is in the ideal position to maintain current awareness of the range of information sources available and the best way to exploit them.

In responding to any enquiry, the librarian will, of course, need to use her professional judgement to decide whether the same information could be obtained at less cost from another source. For instance, a journal article might be obtained through the public library network or from a neighbouring school library. Information on foreign exchange rates, accessible on the Prestel database, is also published in most daily newspapers. The librarian will need to weigh the staff time and other factors involved in acquiring materials by conventional means against the online costs and professional time involved in searching Campus. For the experienced user, the system provides rapid and extremely convenient access to information.

Campus 2000 and the future

Campus is a dynamic and constantly changing resource. Any review of what it offers schools can be little more than a snapshot of the system at a particular stage in its development.

A number of recent projects have focused on improved links with European schools. These include EDU2000, a pilot scheme linking schools in Britain and France. From April 1992 Campus users will be able to access the Teletel online system operated by the French Education Ministry. A similar project will link 25 British schools with their counterparts in Catalonia, Spain. In addition, a growing number of schools from Germany, Austria, Scandinavia and Russia are joining the network and taking part in collaborative work using electronic mail and conferencing.

Future developments within British Telecom will allow new products and services to be offered, exploiting satellite, fibre optic and other emerging technologies. Specific areas already being investigated by Campus 2000 include the facility to send fax and telex messages from electronic mailboxes; links to the Spanish education online service 'AGORA'; improvements to the conferencing system and work to allow Campus subscribers to communicate with users on other networks. The overall result should be greatly enhanced communications systems for schools within the near future. All subscribers will benefit from more extensive networking facilities and more user-friendly access methods and software.

Campus 2000 offers pupils, librarians and teachers access to a 'real world' communications system. It helps them to solve their information needs and allows them to communicate with other users anywhere on the network. Campus extends the range of information sources available within school and provides pupils with fresh audiences for their work.

Online systems such as Campus 2000 have a role to play in education far beyond simply allowing students to develop their skills in handling new technology. They have an important contribution to make to the information skills curriculum, enabling pupils to grow into confident and independent learners.

References

1 Marland, M., *Information skills in the secondary curriculum*, Schools Council, 1981.
2 Markless, S. and Lincoln, P., *Tools for learning: information skills and learning to learn in secondary schools*, British Library, 1986.
3 Sansom, S., *Campus 2000 user guide*, British Telecom, 1991.
4 Condon, J., *Letting the information world into your school: the use of the modem*, Library Association School Libraries Group, 1987.

7 CD-ROM in the school library

Shirley Matthews

Introduction

CD-ROM has been called 'one of the most exciting developments in educational IT'[1] and it has revolutionized the way information is stored and retrieved. The number of titles available increases almost daily and has risen from about 70–80 titles in 1986 to over 2,000 in 1992.[2]

CD-ROMs are Compact Disks – Read Only Memory. This means that the information stored on the disks can be read but not altered. The disks look exactly like audio CDs but can contain information stored in the form of text, images and maps as well as sound (e.g. music). The information is stored digitally as a series of pits in the surface of the disc and read by a laser which is housed in a special CD-ROM drive connected to a computer. One CD-ROM can store a vast amount of information – equivalent to 1,500 floppy disks or 300,000 pages of A4 text. This means that the entire contents of a 21-volume encyclopedia or the text of a newspaper for a whole year can be held on one CD-ROM disc. Each disc has its own search and retrieval programs and searching is very fast and flexible. Searches may be made by using combinations of keywords; cross-referencing is very simple and the results of a search can be printed out or downloaded to floppy disks for future use.

The titles available include bibliographic data, e.g. BOOKBANK (Whitaker's *British books in print*) and BNB (*British national bibliography*); encyclopedias, e.g. *Grolier electronic encyclopedia, Hutchinson's encyclopedia* and *World book information finder*; atlases, e.g. *Software Toolworks electronic world atlas*; and newspapers, e.g. *Times/Sunday Times, Guardian, Independent* and *Northern echo*. A recent development is the 1981 census on CD-ROM and there are dictionaries, directories and libraries of clip-art images which can be imported into desktop publishing packages.

CD-ROM also provides an alternative means of accessing external databases without the cost of telephone charges. ECCTIS (Educational Counselling and Credit Transfer Information Service) provides information about courses in further and higher education in the United Kingdom. NERIS (National Educational Resources Information Service) includes information on a wide variety of learning and teaching resources. Both these services were previously only available as online services, accessed by using a computer and a modem linked to a telephone line.

As so many CD-ROM titles contain the text of reference books or newspapers, they have immediate applications in a school library. Increasingly, school librarians and teachers have been using microcomputers to exploit the resources in the school library and to gain access to information held on external databases such as ECCTIS and NERIS, via online services. The arrival of CD-ROM has meant that pupils can now have permanent access to full-text information sources in the school library. For the teacher, CD-ROM provides an extensive range of sources which can be used in the curriculum and can, in some cases, greatly improve the quality of work done by pupils. For the librarian, CD-ROM extends the range of resources available in the school library and further allows the educationally valuable interchange of print and electronic media by pupils in the library.

Hardware and software

As previously described, CD-ROM disks are 12cm silvered disks which are read by a laser beam housed in a CD-ROM drive. Some computers have built-in CD-ROM drives which replace one of the conventional floppy disk drives but most drives are a separate unit which is attached to the microcomputer by a lead. The micro-computer has to be fitted with a special interface card and specialized software must be installed, e.g. MSDEX (Microsoft CD-ROM Extensions).

Some CD-ROM drives have a drawer or tray which slides out for the disk to be inserted but most drives require the use of a plastic caddy. The disk is put into the caddy and the caddy is inserted into the drive. Opening and closing the caddy is time-consuming and it is sensible to store each CD-ROM disk in its own caddy. This also helps to protect the disk. A CD-ROM lens cleaner, which is a CD with a small brush attached, can be purchased to run through the drive periodically.

Most CD-ROM disks now conform to a world-wide standard known as ISO 9660, but not all CD-ROM disks will run on all machines. The majority of CD-ROM titles are published for IBM PC microcomputers or compatibles which run MS-DOS, or for Apple Macintosh computers. CD-ROMs may also be used with Acorn Archimedes and Commodore Amiga computers by using a

PC Emulator – software which enables these computers to run MS-DOS applications. IBM PC or compatible machines should be PC-286 or PC-386 and have at least 1 megabyte of RAM (Random Access Memory) but preferably 2 megabytes. This is becoming essential for disks which run under the Windows environment. The microcomputer should have a Winchester hard disk drive which is at least 20 megabytes and preferably 40 megabytes or more, a VGA (Video Graphics Array) colour monitor and a printer. Librarians and teachers in schools with no previous experience of the hardware and software needed to run CD-ROM applications would be well advised to consult other schools or libraries which already use CD-ROMs before committing themsleves to purchasing hardware which might limit their future use of CD-ROMs.

The information on most CD-ROMs can be accessed by inserting the disk into the drive and typing the name of the title or a simple command. Some CD-ROM tiles, however, come with a floppy disk which contains installation and search and retrieval programs. These programs have to be copied on to the computer's hard disk before the CD-ROM can be used. Setting up the microcomputer and installing the software is still not an easy task, although it is less complicated than it used to be. School librarians and teachers installing interface boards and CD-ROM software should take professional advice, perhaps from the school's information technology specialists in order to avoid complications. Increasingly, CD-ROM applications come in turnkey systems, i.e. complete, ready-to-operate systems which include a microcomputer with an interface board fitted, a CD-ROM drive, the CD-ROM software installed and a selection of CD-ROM disks set up and ready to run.

CD-ROM systems are still relatively expensive and most schools will only be able to afford one system, which will normally be held in the school library. Networking CD-ROMs (see below) is still, for schools, fairly new and expensive. If there is only one system in the library, it will soon be in constant use. A printer is an essential part of a CD-ROM system in that it allows pupils to print out the results of their searches, take the printout away and incorporate the findings of their search into their own work. A printout can also be used by a teacher as a basis for discussion by a group of pupils. In one Hertfordshire school, a teacher encourages special needs pupils to highlight the words they do not understand in their printout and then explains them later as part of the general group discussion. Searches can also be downloaded on to floppy disks. This allows pupils to take their disk and manipulate the information they have retrieved on a word-processing package either in the classroom or in the library.

CD-ROM titles

The Grolier electronic encyclopedia

The first and still the most popular encyclopedia on CD-ROM, *Grolier* is a 21-volume American encyclopedia. The 1991 edition on CD-ROM contains the text of over 30,000 articles, pictures and maps. Accompanying the articles are many tables, factboxes and extensive bibliographies. Searches can be made for any word or words and there are Browse Titles and Browse Word Index facilities. Certain names, titles, words and phrases are cross-referenced and references can be followed up by moving to related articles elsewhere in the encyclopedia, using a hypertext facility.

One of the novel features of encyclopedias on CD-ROM is the availability of sound which accompanies articles, e.g. on the speeches of Martin Luther King; the music of composers such as Beethoven; and the songs of different species of bird. For UK pupils and teachers, there are slight disadvantages in the use of American spelling and the bias towards the history and geography of the USA but the advantages of having this kind of source of information in a form which is far more easily searched than in hard copy far outweigh the disadvantages. *Grolier* is also published on CD-ROM as the *Software Toolworks New illustrated encyclopedia* and appears in many different CD-ROM drive and disk bundles. Figure 7.1[3] shows the use made of *Grolier* in the school library by pupils and teachers at Ashlyns School during a typical school week. Figure 7.1 shows not only the wide range of topics searched for but also how *Grolier* was used by pupils ranging from Year 3 to Year 6. The searches outlined below were made as part of the normal curricular activities of pupils and were not chosen at random, to allow pupils to have experience of using a CD-ROM system.

Day/Period	Topic	Subject	Year
Monday 3/4	Plate tectonics	Geography	6
Monday 5/6	Natural hazards	Geography 6	
Tuesday 4	Inflation	Economics	5
Tuesday 8	Third World countries	Geography	3
Tuesday 3.30	Camus	Research by Languages Dept	
Wednesday 3	Modern authors	English Open Studies	5
Wednesday 4	Alternative energy	CDT	3
Thursday 6	Explorers	History	6
Thursday 7	Migration	Geography	4
Friday 4	Drugs	Health Studies	6
Friday 5	Sutton Hoo burial	History	3

Fig. 7.1

World book information finder
This encyclopedia is based on the well-known *World book encyclopedia* and contains over 17,000 articles. There are no pictures or sound in the current edition but future editions are likely to have this facility. There is a dictionary facility which can be consulted without losing the original search and there are links to related topics. The text is suitable for secondary (12 – 18 years) and middle-school (9 – 13 years) pupils and may be printed or downloaded to disk.

NERIS
NERIS is well known to teachers and librarians and has been available online for several years. The CD-ROM version, which is much easier to use than its online counterpart, runs under the GEM operating system and uses pull-down menus and a mouse and will soon be available running under Windows 3. NERIS contains details of over 40,000 teaching and learning resources including fact sheets, work sheets, journal articles, details of computer software, educational broadcasts and teacher-produced materials. The database can be searched by subject, age, phase, media, title or publisher and is annotated for the National Curriculum. NERIS on CD-ROM is available as an annual subscription which entitles the subscriber to three updated disks per year. While NERIS is primarily geared towards use by teachers, senior pupils working on extensive projects also use NERIS. In Ashlyns School, for example, NERIS was used by Social Education teachers to search for suitable posters on human nutrition and by Year 6 pupils searching for information on the famine in Sudan for Community Studies and on the UK's hi-tech industries for Technology Studies.[4]

ECCTIS
ECCTIS 2000 is a UK courses information service which provides details of over 81,000 courses in universities, polytechnics and further education colleges. Searches may be made in relation to subject, type of course, institution and location. Course details provided include entry requirements and information about the institution providing the course. The ECCTIS CD-ROM now also provides information for school governors, Department of Education and Science circulars and governor's guides. ECCTIS is available as an annual subscription which provides three updated disks each year.

Software Toolworks World atlas
This comprehensive atlas on CD-ROM includes over 200 full-colour maps of the world, regions, countries and oceans. Pupils can search

for information, including statistics, on subjects such as governments, crime, inflation rates, climate, environment and time zones. Statistics can be displayed in different kinds of graphs and both maps and statistics can be printed out. Figure 7.2 shows a printout of a map relating to life expectancy for females across the world and Figure 7.3 shows a printout of information on the same topic in graph form. The great advantage for both pupils and teachers of having an atlas in CD-ROM format is that sample maps and statistical tables can be printed out and included in the pupils' work, thus adding to the quality of both the content and the presentation of the work.

The Times/Sunday Times

This CD-ROM contains the full text of both newspapers on one disk. The updated disks are issued quarterly and the final disk covers the whole of the previous year. The 1992 disk contains photographs as well as text. The information can be searched by date, section of the paper (e.g. sport, home news), headline, byline and text. Searches can be made by using keywords or phrases. Figure 7.4 shows the results of a search made for information on animal rights in a Hertfordshire school and Figure 7.5 shows a range of articles found as a result of this search.

1981 Census

This CD-ROM contains boundary maps at ward level for Great Britain, all district, county and national summaries, mid-1987 population statistics and all small area statistics. One slight drawback of using the 1981 Census on CD-ROM is that it requires Windows 3 to be used.

CD-ROM in school libraries

By 1988 CD-ROMs, both bibliographic and full text, were in use mainly in academic and special libraries. There was, however, no documented use of CD-ROM in schools. In September 1988, a two-year research project, funded by the British Library, was set up to investigate the potential of CD-ROMs in school libraries, with particular emphasis on their educational value and relevance to the curriculum. The project also looked at CD-ROM as an alternative to online information services available to schools. As part of the project, CD-ROM workstations were installed in two secondary schools in Hertfordshire and in the Schools Library Service HQ. A wide range of disks was compared and the final report analysed their use by pupils and teachers and their value to a range of curricular subjects.

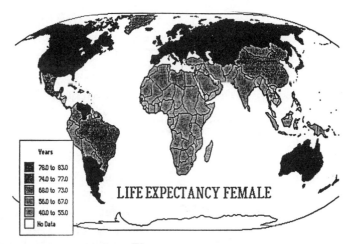

Fig. 7.2 *Source: World atlas*ᵀᴺ, published by The Software Toolworks, Inc., 60 Leveroni Court, Novato, CA 94949. ©1989, 1990, 1991 Electromap Inc., pob 1153, Fayetteville, AR 72702. Data are reproduced with permission from various United Nation and other international sources. A complete list of sources is included in the program and user guide.

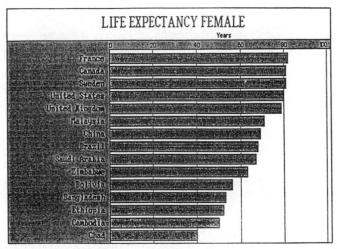

Fig. 7.3 *Source: World atlas* ᵀᴹ, published by The Software Toolworks, Inc., 60 Leveroni Court, Novato, CA 94949. ©1989, 1990, 1991 Electromap Inc., pob 1153, Fayetteville, AR 72702. Data are reproduced with permission from various United Nation and other international sources. A complete list of sources is included in the program and user guide.

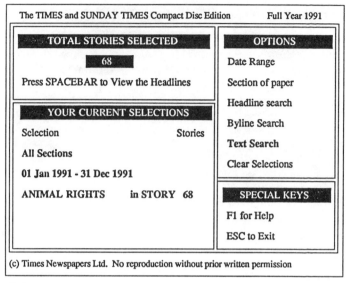

Fig. 7.4

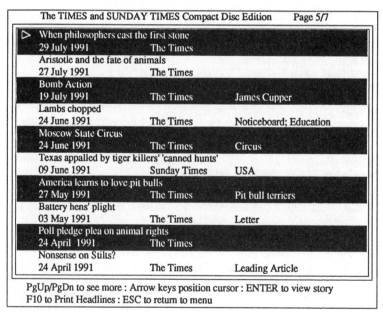

Fig. 7.5

The findings of the project showed that CD-ROM was an invaluable source of information in the school library, which stimulated further research among pupils and reinforced the importance of information-handling skills for pupils. The relevance of the CD-ROMs to the curriculum, however, depended on the content of the disks available and the level and range of information provided. The report *CD-ROMs in school libraries*[4] also made recommendations to publishers, to the manufacturers of equipment, to headteachers and to curriculum planners in schools in relation to the range of disks which might be made available to schools, the ease of use of hardware and software and the potential of CD-ROM in the curriculum.

Since that report was published, the number of CD-ROM systems in schools around the country has risen dramatically. In Hertfordshire alone, there are now 50 schools with CD-ROM in their school libraries. This increase has been partly due to government funding and national initiatives such as the NCET/DES CD-ROM pilot scheme but many schools have also invested TVEI money and funds raised by PTAs to purchase CD-ROM drives and disks.

Information skills and the National Curriculum
Experience in the use of CD-ROM by pupils in schools has underlined the importance of information-handling skills. The British Library Report commented that all the CD-ROM titles investigated were different – they all required different search procedures. There was no one set of rules which always applied – the procedures for combining search terms varied from CD-ROM to CD-ROM, and each had to be learnt and remembered. Some had browsing facilities, some were approached via a thesaurus or a word list. Searches could be constructed using Boolean operators AND, OR, NOT. Some used a mouse to search, some operated under Windows and used pull-down menus.

Successful searches depended on the planning of search strategies before looking for information. It was vital to know what sort of information each CD-ROM title was likely to produce and to select the most likely source of information. Search terms and keywords had to be listed before using the CD-ROMs and search strategies modified and changed as the search progressed. It was observed that pupils worked best in small groups, discussing their problems and ideas, planning searches and learning from one another.

The importance of information-handling skills is emphasized by the National Curriculum. Pupils are 'required to become sophisticated information handlers', to possess a range of skills and 'an appreciation of the concepts underlying information storage and use'.[5] Pupils must be able to select information from a wide range of sources, evaluate, synthesize, record and present the information.

The National Curriculum also stresses the cross-curricular use of IT. Pupils must be able to locate information in databases, use IT for storage and retrieval of information, organize and present ideas using IT and understand the uses of a range of devices for handling information and communication.

Information skills are referred to in the document sent out by NCET at the time of the NCET/DES CD-ROM Pilot Scheme in Schools in 1991. It states that the successful use of CD-ROM demands particular information-handling skills, and the medium therefore has considerable potential for helping to develop these skills.

CD-ROM and the National Curriculum – some examples and applications

In Mathematics, pupils are required to 'extract specific pieces of information from tables and lists' (Key Stage 3 AT 13/29), and 'to present a set of complex data in a variety of diagrams and graphs' (Key Stage 4 AT 12 26).

The 1981 Census CD-ROM, the *World atlas* and even the *Guinness disc of records* all provide a wealth of statistical data and raw material for this purpose – population and climate statistics, inflation rates, literacy figures, etc.

The Census and *Atlas* CD-ROMs would also provide statistical data for Geography. Census returns are referred to in IT and History documents, and pupils are required to analyse the results of surveys for Technology and Geography.

Pupils are also required 'to use a large database about careers or courses, and refine techniques of enquiry to select relevant information' (IT Level 7 AT 5). ECCTIS on CD-ROM would provide this database.

Newspapers are mentioned in the English National Curriculum documents. Pupils are required to 'recognise the structure of news stories or the ways in which television programmes and newspapers match style and content to a specific audience' (English: Reading: Level 9 AT 2). They are asked to 'compare the presentation of news' and to 'compare the treatment of the same event in two newspapers' (English Reading: Level 10 AT 2). The newspapers on CD-ROM, which now include the *Times/Sunday Times*, the *Independent*, the *Guardian* and the *Northern echo*, would provide invaluable sources of information. In particular, the new 'Snapshot in Time' CD-News disk from Research Machines and Attica, would be very relevant to these requirements. The disk contains articles and photographs from the *Independent* and *Independent on Sunday*, the *Daily mail* and the *Mail on Sunday*, the *Observer*, the *European* and *Le monde* for the month of August 1991. It is possible to display articles from two different newspapers on the screen at the same time. Events in August 1991 included the failed Russian coup, fighting in Yugoslavia, the release of John McCarthy and the first anniversary of the invasion of Kuwait.

There are many other examples. NCET have published some excellent curriculum support materials which contain practical ideas for using CD-ROMs in subject courses, linking topics to the National Curriculum. The materials include four booklets on NERIS, ECCTIS, encyclopedias and newspapers on CD-ROM. They all emphasize the importance of information skills and the planning of search strategies.

CD-ROM use in Hertfordshire schools

In Hertfordshire most schools have had their CD-ROM systems for at least a year now, although some schools have only recently acquired machines. A recent survey (January 1992) was conducted to obtain details of the equipment and disks in schools and, more importantly, to show how CD-ROM was being used to support the curriculum.

The most popular CD-ROM titles are still the *Grolier encyclopedia*, NERIS, ECCTIS and the *Times/Sunday Times* disks, followed closely by the *World atlas*. Several schools are now buying a second newspaper on CD-ROM and some have the Library of the Future disk which is included in the Research Machines bundle. A variety of other disks have been purchased by individual schools, including the 1981 Census disk, the *Financial Times*, the McGraw-Hill Reference Set, the *Guinness disc of records* and the *Complete Shakespeare* on CD-ROM.

In some schools, formal training sessions are arranged for both teachers and pupils. Training for teachers may be held as part of official INSET days, at departmental or faculty meetings or on an individual basis after school. One school organizes sessions for staff during an annual resources review for each subject held during the summer examination period. New staff are also introduced to CD-ROM when they join the school.

Pupils may be shown CD-ROM in small groups, given a general introduction which is followed up with help on an individual basis when the CD-ROMs are being used. In one school an Economics teacher trained his own GCSE and A-level groups to use the *Times/Sunday Times* disk. First-year Library and Information Skills courses include the use of CD-ROM.

CD-ROM was used regularly as part of coursework in most subject lessons including English, History, Geography, Science and Careers and also in Mathematics, Music, IT, PSE, Business Studies, European Studies and Classics. Librarians reported that many pupils also used CD-ROMs for their own personal interest during the lunch-hour and after school.

The topics researched and the CD-ROMs used make interesting reading and provide further evidence that CD-ROM is an invaluable source of information in the school library. Figure 7.6 shows part of the results of the survey in relation to the different topics searched for by year groups using different CD-ROMs.

Years 7-12 = secondary school pupils aged 13-18)

	Topic	Source
Geography		
A-level	Natural disasters	*Financial Times*
A-level	Inner cities	*Times*
Year 12	Rain forests & deserts	*Grolier*
Year 10	Farming & agriculture	*World atlas*
Year 9	European tourist assignment	*World atlas*
Year 9	Third World projects	*Times*
	– Bangladesh floods, famine	
Year 7	Farming	*Grolier*
History		
Year 12	United Nations	*Grolier*
	George III	
	Disraeli	
Year 9	Canals	NERIS
Year 7	Romans, Roman Britain	*Grolier*
European Studies		
Year 11	Yugoslavia	*Times*
	Baltic Republics	*Times*
English		
Year 12	Drink-driving	*Times/Grolier*
Year 12	Nostradamus	*Grolier*
Year 10	Punishment and crime	*Grolier*
Year 10	Fox-hunting and animal rights	*Times*
	Euthanasia	*Times*
Year 10	Premature babies/	*Times*
	intensive care	
Year 10	Catherine Cookson	*Northern Echo*
Year 9	Animal cruelty	*Times*
	Civil rights	*Grolier/Times/*NERIS
	Black America	*Grolier/Times*
Year 8	Caribbean region	*World Atlas*

(cont.)

Religious Studies
Year 11	Drugs	NERIS/*Grolier*
	Enlightenment	*Grolier*
Year 10	Sunday trading	*Times*
	Celibacy and clergy	*Times*
Year 9	India	*Grolier*
Year 8	Turin shroud	*Times*

Physics
A-level	Thermodynamics	McGraw-Hill
A-level	Project ideas	NERIS

Biology
Year 12	Stick insects	NERIS

Science
Year 7	Chernobyl	*Grolier/Times*
Year 7	Archimedes	*Grolier*

Maths
Year 9	Statistics on road traffic accidents	*Times*

Economics
A-level	ERM	*Financial Times*
Year 10	Council tax v. poll tax discursive essays	*Times*

Home Economics
Year 12	Diet/Nutrition	NERIS

Technology
Year 7	Food	*Grolier*
Year 8	Recycling	

Design
Year 7	Roof racks	NERIS
	Gulf oil spills	*Times*

Art
Year 12	Famous artists *Grolier*

Music
Year 12	Coursework – performers, concert halls	*Times*
Year 8	'Call and response'	*Grolier*

PSE
Year 7/8	Elections and political parties	*Northern Echo*
Year 7/8	Homelessness	*Times*
Year 10	Environmental issues	NERIS

(cont.)

General Studies

Year 10/11	Child development	*Grolier*/NERIS
	Pregnancy	
	Hormones	
	Handicapped children	
	Development of sight and	
	hearing	
	Topics for debate	*Times*

Cross-curricular themes

Year 12	Politics	*Times*
Year 10	Gulf War	*Times*
Year 9	Russia	*Hutchinson*
	Current affairs	
	− the Russian Revolution	*Times*
Year 12	History diary of 1991	*Times*

(Sixth-form students have to produce a diary of events for four weeks at beginning of 1991 and then follow it up six months later)

Fig. 7.6

The future

Government initiatives

The NCET/DES CD-ROM Pilot Scheme in 1991 made £500,000 available for LEAs to encourage the use of CD-ROM in schools. Each LEA was allocated a share of the grant to buy CD-ROM equipment and disks and selected schools were asked to take part in a pilot study. Suppliers and manufacturers were invited to send products to NCET who produced a list of recommended disks and drives for the LEAs. NCET sent out very detailed specifications to interested suppliers, and the recommendations made in the British Library Report in 1990 asking for easy-to-install drives and software, on-screen instructions and simple manuals, were all included.

In 1992 the DES included money for CD-ROM in its Grants for Education Support and Training (GEST) for 1992–3 which provided 40 per cent funding (£1.6 million) for a £4 million project to put a CD-ROM drive into every secondary school. LEAs will have to provide a total of £2.4 million to match the DES funding. Again, NCET's list of approved players and disks will form the basis for LEA bids.

Networking

CD-ROM networks are still relatively new in schools. A computer with a CD-ROM drive acts as a dedicated server and is linked to an existing network. Special software is needed to establish this link. A network licence has to be obtained for each CD-ROM title used and the network version of a CD-ROM is usually much more expensive than the stand-alone version.

If only one CD-ROM drive is linked to the network, the users will only be able to search one CD-ROM, and use the same disk at the same time. This means that the disk will need to be changed manually. School librarians could find themselves responsible for changing the disks for network users, if the server is located in the school library and unable to use the CD-ROM title of their own choice. A more satisfactory example is a network with a stack or tower of six CD-ROM drives attached allowing users to access any one of six different disks. Disks are selected automatically when a user wishes to search a particular disk.

There should always be at least one stand-alone CD-ROM machine in the school library and eventually another machine, or even a small network.

New titles
New titles are becoming available all the time, but there are still gaps in the type and content of information available on CD-ROM. Indexes to periodicals such as the *New scientist* would be very useful, as would world geographical data and statistics for older pupils. There is a need for a science encyclopedia for the lower-school and younger pupils. A 'How it works'-type encyclopedia of science and invention on CD-ROM with illustrations, diagrams, working models and animated sequences would be invaluable for CDT and the National Curriculum. A good general, preferably British, junior encyclopedia such as the *Oxford children's encyclopedia* is long overdue on CD-ROM.

Conclusion
The Guidance Document sent out by NCET describes CD-ROMs as 'whole-school resources' which are usually located in a library or resources centre. It comments that 'in this setting they are supervised by library or resources staff, and students are able to use CD-ROM information as a part of their work in any subject'. It suggests that 'using CD-ROMs also encourages wider and better quality use of other information resources'.[6]

CD-ROM is very exciting. It allows fast access to a wealth of information. Children find it attractive and fun to use. The amount of information retrieved can be daunting, however, and planned and structured searching is essential. Information-handling skills are vital.

Since CD-ROM is a source of information and reference material, the obvious location for the CD-ROM system is in the school library. Some disks contain subject-specific materials and are more relevant to one particular subject area. In this case, a CD-ROM system might be located in a classroom used by one subject department. In general, however, more students will have access to CD-ROM if the systems are housed in the school library. As with all other resources in the library, their use in the context of the curriculum should be planned and developed by teachers and librarian working together. Only then will the full potential of CD-ROM be explored and exploited as a resource for learning.

References

1 Mapp, L., 'Knowledge at your fingertips', *Teachers' weekly*, 7 March 1991.
2 *CD-ROMs in print 1992*, Meckler, 1992.
3 Royce, C. *et al.*, *CD-ROM: usage and prospects*, British Library, 1989, (British Library Report 71).
4 Matthews, S., *CD-ROMs in school libraries*, British Library, 1990, (BLR&DD Report 6001).
5 *Information skills and the National Curriculum*, NCET, 1990.
6 *CD-ROM resources list*, NCET/DES Pilot Scheme for CD-ROM in Schools, July 1991.

8 Selecting software in schools

Nigel Akers

Introduction
When teachers and librarians choose books for use in school they
instinctively

- judge their applicability to the curriculum
- assess their reading levels
- check their usefulness within the contexts of structure and
  layout
- decide whether or not to purchase them on the basis of cost,
  need and comparison with other books already in school.

All this they do regularly, and often without consulting colleagues
– lengthy deliberations are not generally the order of the day. And
whether the books would fit on the shelves is of no consequence
– books *do* fit on shelves.

In the world of computer software selection though, there is a
whole new language to be understood, a whole new set of
procedures to be dealt with to obtain what might be of use, and
whole new chapters to be written in books like this. Or so it would
seem. In reality, the process is no different than it should be for
purchasing books. Selecting any materials should be a collaborative
process to ensure that decisions about purchasing new stock are
based upon the needs of the school, the suitability of the title and
its 'cost effectiveness': the things that are instinctively done when
choosing books. Effective selection is important and time-
consuming. If it is carried out by individuals, instinctively, time may
be saved, but at what expense to the education of pupils, and to
the school budget? Perhaps it is because single items of software
are often that much more expensive than books that teachers and
librarians recognize the need for such collaboration.

Collaborative procedures should, and in many cases do, exist in
schools for the purchase of software (and other materials) in
recognition of these concerns, and should be seen as a positive move
towards the improvement of materials selection. There should be,

and often is, a written selection policy, containing guidelines and evaluative criteria, to assist those deciding on purchases. The exact nature of the collaboration will vary from school to school – it may be a committee of staff members, it may be the senior management team, it may include parent, pupil or governor representatives. Whichever format is decided upon, a procurement coordinator will be required, someone who will coordinate requests, order materials and ensure their accessibility upon receipt, as well as ensure that the objective criteria and evaluation procedures written in the selection policy are applied to those requests – all tasks that fall within the training and experience of chartered librarians.

The following factors should be taken into account by such coordinators:

- the needs of the curriculum
- knowledge of existing software in school
- knowledge of available software
- technical specifications
- financial implications
- future developments.

Choosing software for the curriculum
Before any decisions are made about the purchase of software for use in school, the procurement coordinator and the selection committee should have a clear idea of the fundamental philosophy of the school in relation to information technology, and of the curriculum and syllabuses followed within the school.

Considerations which will determine the IT philosophy of the school, and which should be included in the selection policy, could include the adherence to one particular platform (e.g. Windows 3.0 software) or the exclusion of particular types of software, such as games. Decisions will need to be taken about progression to accommodate students of all ages and abilities. Should, for example, a whole range of word-processing packages be made available, or would one or two suffice? How many CD-ROM titles should be purchased, if only one CD-ROM drive exists in school? It may be more cost-effective to purchase an additional drive rather than an additional disk. Are software packages being bought because they cover a topic that is on the syllabus, or because they will be used in the curriculum? Have the logistics of using such curricular packages been thought through? Are alternative packages available? If the school has computers that are networked, will the software operate on that network? Is the software allowed to be operated over the network?

An awareness of the syllabuses and curriculum being followed is essential to avoid being blinded by the wonder and wizardry of many software packages now on the market. Virgin Interactive's *North Polar expedition*[1] on CD-ROM or interactive video is a superb resource, but if it is not going to be used within the curriculum it may be a waste of money. The elements of information technology capability in the (English and Welsh) National Curriculum, contained within Attainment Target 5 of Technology in the National Curriculum,[2] include areas, or 'strands' such as modelling and information handling, which need to be assessed across the whole curriculum. To satisfy these requirements, students will need access to spreadsheet and database software, databanks and CD-ROM 'encyclopedias' as simple to manipulate as *PC globe* (available in the UK from Djanogly CTC) or as detailed as Chadwick-Healey's *Census 1981* on CD-ROM to which additional data can be added and interrogated. By being aware of such requirements, schools can be better assured that software is being selected to best benefit the pupils.

Software awareness
An awareness of the requirements of the curriculum should be complemented by an awareness of the existing software within the school − a thorough annual audit of what is available and what is used is an excellent exercise, particularly where networks exist and space for software is at a premium. Software packages exist, such as Roderick Manhattan's *Windows workstation*, which will make such tasks that much easier, logging those programs which are used, and enabling informed judgements to be made on which software should be dispensed with or retained.

With such an awareness of both the curriculum and existing software, the task of identifying new software packages to be purchased is made that much easier. The means of identifying them are identical to the means by which teachers and librarians identify new books to be purchased:

- product literature and software catalogues
- NERIS, and product reviews in journals and magazines
- exhibitions and demonstrations.

Product literature from software houses is the most prolific and glossy source of information on the very latest software products. Once they are aware of the hardware base within a school (gleaned from a few requests for further details of specific software titles) there will be no shortage, even in the depths of a recession, of enticements to spend money on their products. If producers are not promoting their wares direct, the software retailers are doing it indirectly. Few schools can have missed AVP's *Big black catalogue* which covers most of the educational software for the four hardware platforms – it does not, however, list much of the PC-based industry-standard software, for which guides like Action Computer Supplies software catalogue (Freefone 0800 333333) are invaluable. Subject-specific guides make the tracking down of suitable software packages that much easier – examples include ALBSU's *Basic skills software guide* and NCET's *Careers software review*. Published (and therefore often costly) guides such as Whitaker/NCET's *Educational software*, TFPL's *The CD-ROM directory* and VNU Business Publications' *PC yearbook*, will ensure that no reputable piece of software is missed, provided the annual or bi-annual editions can be afforded. Given the move towards PC software, another useful guide, complete with details of educational discounts aimed at further and higher education but applicable to secondary schools, is the *CHEST software directory* published by Bath University Press.

NERIS (the National Educational Resources Information Service) provides a more in-depth guide to what is available for schools. Although its coverage of educational software is not comprehensive, the details on NERIS (which is available either 'on-line' or on CD-ROM) do offer schools not only details of software titles, producers, suppliers and price, but also age-range applicability, subject coverage by keywords and technical specifications and reviews. These reviews, however, are often provided by the software suppliers and so should be treated with caution. Independent reviews of software can be found in a variety of journals and magazines, from the BBC's *Educational computing & technology* and similar house journals, to MUSE's *Information technology and learning*, and the Computer Education Group's journal, *Computer education*. Computing updates in the *Times educational supplement*, reviews in the *School Libraries Group news* and in a wide range of computing magazines add to the whole complicated business – to read wildly differing reviews of the same product on a variety of pages is a common feature in the world of software evaluation. Buyer beware!

To be convinced of the value of a particular software package, the product is best seen in operation – if possible in school by obtaining a copy on approval, or second best by trialling it at an exhibition, demonstration event or at a local school that has already purchased a copy. Major exhibitions of the latest software products are a regular feature at Olympia, the Barbican or the National Exhibition Centre – and entry is usually free. The year starts with the BETT exhibition in January, followed by Computers in Libraries in February, the Education Show in March/April, Multimedia 92 (93, 94, etc.) in June, the Library Technology Fair (at Hatfield

Polytechnic) in September, TIME (The Interactive Media Event) in October and Online 92 (93, 94, etc.) in December. Do not assume, however, that what is being demonstrated at such events is what the final sale version of the product will be. One of the leading newspaper titles on CD-ROM was demonstrated from a hard disk, rather than a CD-ROM, at Online 90. The School Libraries Group of the Library Association organized events such as the 'Hands on ... CD-ROM and DVI' workshops (e.g. in May and October 1992 at Djanogly CTC) to further aid those in search of help and advice, to provide training in the use of software packages and to improve awareness of the range of products and future developments.

That professionals, be they teachers or librarians, should require training and familiarization with software packages should not be underestimated. Indeed, the key to the success or failure of any software item lies in the confidence with which staff can introduce it into the curriculum. User-friendliness is a much-maligned term in the software business, but it is crucial. School librarians and teachers should look for GUI software (icon-driven Graphical User Interfaces that can be 'clicked' on to effect a result). They should also look for on-screen help and on-screen tutorials. User manuals are often a good guide to the reliability of the software. If the manual appears to be extremely complicated, it may be that the software is unsuitable or it may be that more technical help is needed to identify the actual uses of this software in the school.

Technical specifications
In UK schools at present there are four main types of computer hardware. In Scotland, Apple computers dominate the education market. In England and Wales, following Government initiatives in the early 1980s which locked schools into 'education' computers from either the BBC or Research Machines range, Archimedes and Nimbus computers have the greatest market share. Increasingly, however, PCs (IBM-compatible Personal Computers operating under MS-DOS or Windows 3.0) are making their mark in schools, and some local education authorities, such as Shropshire, have adopted this type of industry-based machine as standard in their schools. This trend will continue with the fall in price of PCs, with the cooperation of IBM and Apple internationally in future developments of hardware, with the Government support of CD-ROM initiatives in schools (CD-ROMs having been developed primarily within the PC environment) and with both Acorn and Research Machines producing machines that not only operate under their own disk-operating systems but also can emulate, and thus run programs written for, PCs.

The procurement coordinator and selection committee must become familiar with the technical terms that abound in relation to the software that will (or will not) run on whichever hardware type or types exist within the school. In the early days of BBC 'B' computers the only considerations were whether the software was available on a cassette or a floppy disk, and whether the floppy disk was formatted for 40 or 80 tracks or would run over a simple network. Figure 8.1 shows an example of the technical specification that is required today to use all the information contained within one piece of software:

> The minimum equipment you need to be able to use all of *The Multimedia Encyclopedia of mammalian biology* is:
>
> - an IBM compatible AT computer (an 80286 CPU is acceptable but slow; we recommend a 386 SX as the minimum), with a VGA monitor and a 5.25" or 3.5" floppy disk drive
> - 2Mb of RAM (4Mb is recommended)
> - Microsoft Windows 3.0 software, set up for 256 colours with Multimedia Extensions
> - a DVI device driver and DVI i750 Series 2 chipset
> - a hard disk
> - MS-DOS 3.3 or higher
> - an ISO 9660 CD-ROM drive compatible with Microsoft Multimedia Extensions
> - a Microsoft compatible mouse.

(Note that a sound board is required for your PC as part of Multimedia Extensions.)

Fig. 8.1

To discover whether this software will work on the equipment that exists in schools will require some investigation and a little knowledge of the acronyms and abbreviations above, but that effort will pay dividends. There are many pieces of software lying around in schools, unused, because the hardware requirements were not taken into account before purchase; many software packages will only work with a mouse, other software packages will only work if the monitor screen is advanced enough to show colour images (VGA is better than EGA). A 486 machine is better than a 386, which is better than a 286. 186 machines are virtually obsolete now in computing terms. The amount of memory (RAM), particularly in networked workstations, is important – Windows 3.0 packages use up a lot of memory, at least 3 Megabytes (Mb) are required for fault-free operation, particularly if the benefits of operating a number of

Windows 3.0 packages at the same time (multi-tasking) are to be assured. MS-DOS 3.3 and Windows 3.0 are a disk-operating system and an operating environment (from Microsoft (MS), hence MS-DOS) and come as standard with any new PC. The current (Spring 1992) versions are MS-DOS 5.0 and Windows 3.1. Multimedia Extensions, sound boards, and DVI (Digital Video Interactive) device drivers are sets of microchips loaded onto 'boards' or 'cards' which can be slotted into spaces inside the computer to enhance its capabilities – in this case, allowing text, data, sound, photographs and full screen, full-motion (digital TV-type) video images to be displayed on the screen or broadcast through headphones or speakers attached to the computer (a necessary extra not often specified in the hardware requirements above).

Network versions of this encyclopedia are available, allowing up to 100 users to access the CD-ROM at the same time from workstations on a network. Suitable CD-ROM networking software (e.g. Optinet), as well as the computer networking software (e.g. Novell or RM-net), is required to make use of this additional facility.

If there is still any doubt about whether or not a particular piece of software will operate with known hardware configurations, school librarians and teachers should seek clarifications from the suppliers or ask for a 28-day trial – suppliers have not been keen to oblige in this respect in the past, but, particularly with CD-ROMs which cannot be 'copied', there are indications that customers' concerns are now forcing a change. McGraw-Hill's *Encyclopedia of mammalian biology* is readily available on 28-day free approval – their *Science and technical reference set* on CD-ROM (version 1) of the late 1980s was not and was beset with problems of hardware compatibility.

Using any new technology will present problems for teachers and school librarians, and technical problems can often be overcome by seeking advice either from technical experts in school (who may not necessarily always be involved in the *selection* of the software) or from experts outside school, such as teacher-training institutions or LIS schools. The important aspect of developing new technologies in schools is the *sharing* of experience within the school amongst teachers and school librarians. Where schools have an IT coordinator, this person is often the one who can refer less experienced staff to the school librarian or to a teacher in order to overcome technical difficulties.

Financial implications

Having discovered a package that is essential for the curriculum, that has been tried and tested and which will operate on the hardware that exists in school, is by no means the end of the story.

There are financial implications which are all too easily ignored. The price quoted for a single software package is usually for a single-user, stand-alone version. If the package is to be run over a network, school staff should check the user licence fees, and read the small print. FAST (the Federation Against Software Theft) has recently discovered large quantities of software being operated from 'illegal' copies in schools in a London Borough. The penalties for such infringement of copyright are huge. A check should also be made for software 'maintenance' fees – under which telephone support (particularly for products such as school and library administration packages) and updated versions of the software are provided. School librarians and teachers should also ensure that updated versions of software packages that are being considered for purchase will not incur the procurement of updated versions of other pieces of software that interface with it. For example, word-processed files created using *Word for windows (Winword) 2.0*, may require additional expense in updating Aldus *Pagemaker 4.0* which had previously accepted files for desk-top publishing created using *Winword 1.0*. For network licence fees, a check should be made as to whether the number of users covered by the licence relates to concurrent users (how many may be using the software at any one time), registered users (the whole school roll) or the number of computer workstations.

Future developments
Although crystal-ball gazing is a difficult talent to add to the list required to carry out the tasks detailed in the previous paragraphs, it is one that has to be taken into account when finally submitting the order for computer software. Acorn produced BBC 'B' microcomputers and sold them in large numbers to schools in the mid-1980s. Within seven years, those machines, and the software to run on them, have been replaced by BBC 'Masters', Archimedes and A5000s. The Research Machines 380Z and 480Z have been replaced by the Nimbus 186, 286 and 386 (with PC-compatibility improving on each occasion). Interactive videos, produced to run with the aid of a BBC Master in the 1980s, are now being produced to run under PC control. CD-ROMs have always been produced for the PC market in the main, though some excellent titles, such as MultiMedia Corporation's *Ecodisc* on CD-ROM are only available, or are often developed first, for Apple Macs, and a number of Archimedes-based RISC-OS CD-ROM titles with video images were released in Spring 1992.

CD-ROM is being enhanced as CD-ROM XA (eXtended Architecture) to allow greater storage capabilities, as CD-I

(Interactive) and DVI (Digital Video Interactive) to allow greater use of sound and motion. Multi-disk players are already on the market to allow standard-size CDs, and smaller or larger (12") laser disks to be played on one machine. DVI, when fully developed, will be able to store vast amounts of data in microchips rather than on CDs, which may negate the additional expense, in years to come, of CD-ROM drives. The potential to access CD-ROMs or DVI products over cable TV telecommunications networks may likewise simplify the hardware requirements at school and in the home, test the creativity of interactive software producers and provide software purchasers with some interesting selection problems. It will never be possible for school librarians to anticipate *all* the changes in hardware and software available on the market, but it is important that they keep up to date by reading relevant articles about educational IT.

Case Study – Djanogly City Technology College

Introduction
The Djanogly City Technology College opened in September 1989 as the country's first purpose-built CTC – an 11–18 community school for students of all abilities living in a tightly defined catchment area in the inner city of Nottingham. Initial capital funding from industry and the Department of Education and Science enabled a fibre-optic network to be installed throughout the College during its building. At the time of opening, discussions were still taking place over which hardware type should be installed – the industry-standard IBM-compatibles to reflect the world of work, or the education-standard Nimbus 186s which could run the wealth of education software developed over the years for BBC-type machines, Research Machines' own software and some software packages that were standard in the PC environment. At the end of the day, 24 Nimbus 186s were purchased to run over a local area network of their own in one classroom, providing the opportunity for IT training, and approximately 50 Apricot 386 workstations to be linked to the network (with thin-wire Ethernet segments branching from the fibre-optic hub), operating under Novell Netware 386 and served by two Apricot 486 file-servers.

IT Development Group
Decisions, at that time, over the purchase of software to run on the two systems, were left to faculties, on the basis of knowledge of educational software used in previous schools. However, it quickly became apparent that the 11-year-olds were forging ahead in terms

of their IT capability through self-supported learning on the Apricot machines that were available throughout the day in the library, and that the Nimbus network was not going to meet their needs in such an environment. Given those early indications, the need to monitor the purchase of software to operate over the Apricot network, and to stop the purchase of any further software for the Nimbus network, became apparent.

An IT Development Group was set up, comprising the Principal, the Deputy Principal, the four Faculty Directors, the Network Manager, the IT Curriculum Coordinator and the Director of Library and Information Services. (From August 1992, the Director of Library and Information Services is responsible for the coordination of learning skills (including IT) in the curriculum and, with the Principal, Deputy Principal and Network Manager, for software procurement.) All decisions about software purchases had to be approved by the IT Development Group, and its members were encouraged to search for PC-equivalent software to replace the BBC-based software that some members of staff were still requesting. For example, the only software available in the UK to operate the Boxford lathe, or the Lego Technic materials in the Technology area, appeared to be BBC-based. A phone call to Lego in Denmark revealed that PC-based control software for their products was available (having been produced for the Australian market). A copy duly arrived from Sydney, and Lego UK have now bowed to the inevitable and will supply it within this country. Boxford, likewise, illustrated a PC-controlled lathe on the cover of their education catalogue, though omitted at that time to offer the PC software to the education market within the catalogue.

The deficiencies of the hardware operating the College's two BBC-based interactive video workstations, and their non-networkability, has further reinforced a move to a 100 per cent PC environment, with the networkable CD-ROM (and the emerging DVI) format as standard. The interactive video players are actually linked to a stand-alone PC to operate MultiMedia Corporation's Gallery series interactive video disks, for television studio simulations (*Eastenders* and *One O'Clock News*).

Windows 3.0 software standard

With the release of Windows 3.0 software, the IT Development Group took the decision that, wherever possible, the software that operated on the network would be Windows-based – a decision that has been vindicated by the results of assessments (in Spring 1992) of Year 7 students (trained on Windows 3.0 packages operating on Apricot 386s) outperforming Year 9 students (trained on the

Nimbus 186s). Microsoft's *Winword* and *Excel* are used as the standard word-processing and spreadsheet packages in generic IT training, with packages such as Roderick Manhattan's *Drafix CAD* used as subject-specific software, also operating under Windows 3.0.

The introduction of students to online systems was awaiting the arrival of Windows-based software. In April 1992, FT Profile launched *Freeway*, a Windows 3.0 software package that enables users to prepare, before logging on, an online search of any of FT Profile's reference, newspaper- and magazine-based databases, to dial up and search, and to automatically download and save all data retrieved. These files can then be word-processed – all within one Windows 3.0, menu-driven, software environment. The ease of access to such information by first-time users is astounding. An additional feature of interest to schools is the capability to limit the cost of any search (to £3.00, for example).

Cross-curricular uses of software

Evidence within subject areas has further shown that the 'simplified' educational software simulations compare unfavourably with the industry-based software packages that can be used in all areas of the curriculum. Information for assignments in 1992 can be accessed from any of the ten CD-ROMs operating over the network of over 100 Apricot 386 workstations, or from a range of disk-based software packages such as *PC Globe*, or *Healthdata*. The CD-ROMs include encyclopedias such as Attica Cybernetic's *Hutchinson's Electronic encyclopedia*, *Dover clip art*, Harrap's *Multilingual dictionaries*, *ECCTIS*, *NERIS*, the *Guinness disc of records*, McGraw-Hill's *Science and technical reference set*, *Europe in the round* and *Food analyst*. All of these CD-ROMs are available from any of the major CD-ROM suppliers. Word-processing, spreadsheet, database and desk-top publishing packages (such as Aldus *Pagemaker 4.0*) can be used to manipulate that information for presentation or interpretation purposes in any subject. Primrose Publishing's *Tick tack* enables students to type in French, Spanish, German or Russian (using the character sets for those languages) for word-processing exercises in their Modern Language lessons.

Assessment at Key Stage 3 of IT capability in the information-handling strand during Spring 1992 has been achieved through pupils logging, on an *Excel* spreadsheet, their use, in any of their lessons, of CD-ROM databases, the *Soutron library system* database, and *PC globe*. Their capability in the modelling strand has similarly involved the use of *Excel* spreadsheets, focused within their mathematics lessons.

Staff are provided with regular opportunities for training in the use of the software packages on the network, either individually (to ensure, for example, that they all have a basic understanding of the packages for which pupils in their lessons may be assessed under the Key Stage 3 assessment procedures), or as faculty or whole-College groups (for example, to ensure that all staff are able to use a newly introduced electronic mail facility).

Future developments
As an extra-curricular activity a number of 11- to 13-year-old students are working on the production of the *Djanogly green energy CD-ROM*, a multi-lingual CD-ROM covering renewable energy technologies, based around European manufacturers' product literature which the students are scanning in and organizing using a Windows 3.0 software package, *Mediabase* – the software used in the production of *Hutchinson's Electronic encyclopedia*. It is hoped to use this product to test the interactivity of Windows packages over cable TV's telecommunications network, linking, potentially, all pupils' homes to the College.

Conclusion
Djanogly CTC is a well-funded, technologically up-to-date school which is perhaps not typical of most UK secondary schools. However, the principles relating to software and hardware selection and use apply in all schools. The importance of coordination in software selection cannot be underestimated. As noted above, many schools have a great deal of software which lies unused in departments because other staff are unaware of its existence. School librarians and teachers can learn from Djanogly's experience in this area and fully exploit even limited software and hardware resources in the school.

References
1 Appendix 1 provides a list of telephone numbers and addresses to contact for the purchase of software referred to.
2 Department of Education and Science, *Technology in the National Curriculum*, HMSO, 1990.

9 Inservice training

Margaret Smith

Introduction

Cambridgeshire Schools Library Service takes a very proactive role in providing an in-depth range of resources and support to all the LEA's primary and secondary schools and now also sells its services to both grant-maintained and independent schools.

Cambridgeshire was one of the counties to pioneer Local Management of Schools (LMS) from the early 1980s and the financial independence of LMS has encouraged many of the schools to respond positively to the advice and support of the Schools Library Service in the development of purpose-built learning resource centres. Cambridge's 46 LEA secondary schools all have a strong commitment to the development of more effective teaching and learning skills through the organization and management of learning resources, including information technology, across the curriculum.

Through the Challenge funding scheme offered to the Schools Library Service, so far 25 schools have appointed professional school librarians in their school resource centres. These initiatives were largely based on support from the Schools Library Service and based on Cambridgeshire LEA guidelines *Provision of learning resources in secondary schools: guidelines for good practice* which were written jointly by the Schools Library Service and Cambridgeshire Education Service.

The Schools Library Service also provides in-depth support to schools without professional librarians. Where teacher-librarians are given a reasonable non-teaching timetable, and the school library is seen as an important part of the school, much work can be achieved in the development of effective learning resource provision. It is much more difficult for schools, even with extensive support and advice from the Schools Library Service, to develop an effective learning resource centre, including whole-curriculum information technology provision, if the commitment provides only for a teacher-librarian with little time to devote to the library and with little funding.

INSET policy

The overall policy on INSET in Cambridgeshire is to provide an intensive and reasonably well-funded programme for schools aimed at developing resource-based learning and teaching in schools, with an emphasis on the development of information skills. It is within this overall framework that INSET directed at the applications of information technology in the school as a whole and in the school library must lie. The use of information technology in schools cannot be separated from developments in the curriculum but should reflect changes in learning and teaching in schools. In order for INSET directed towards information technology in the school to be successful, it will follow on from and support INSET at a more general level.

INSET organized by the Schools Library Service does not exist merely to provide training for school librarians and teacher-librarians. In order for school librarians and teacher-librarians to be effective in schools they will (a) need support from senior management in schools and (b) need to work closely with teachers on developments related to the curriculum including the development of information skills in the use of information technology applications such as the use of databases. Thus part of the strategy of Cambridgeshire Schools Library Service has been to gear INSET as a whole to the development of resource provision and resource-based learning in schools and then to gear INSET to particular aspects such as the use of information technology. This reflects the realities of teachers and librarians working in schools, as any developments which *they* wish to pursue will have to reflect developments in the curriculum as a whole.

INSET in practice

Given the above strategy, the Schools Library Service aimed its INSET in the first instance at the major decision-maker in the school – the headteacher. Virtually all innovations in schools which require extra resources (e.g. new hardware or software in the classroom or in the library) will require support from the headteacher and unless the headteacher is aware of the *context* of innovations directed towards the use of learning resources and the development of information skills, support may not be forthcoming. All school library services are aware of the gaps which exist in the provision of INSET for headteachers, and the management of learning resources and the role of the school librarian do tend to be gaps in this provision.

An INSET day was organized for headteachers with the emphasis on the exploitation of learning resources, which includes computer hardware and software. Figure 9.1 demonstrates the content of the course which the majority of Cambridgeshire's secondary headteachers attended.

ORGANIZATION AND MANAGEMENT
OF
LEARNING RESOURCES IN SECONDARY SCHOOLS

A Schools Library Service Seminar for Headteachers

Aims of the seminar

To provide a forum for headteachers to discuss their views on the Education Department's Consultative Document *The provision of learning resources in secondary schools*

To draw together conclusions about possible developments

The seminar consists of lectures, discussions and group work sessions.

Seminar outline

1.30pm to 2.30pm	Impact of GCSE and TVEI on resource provision and requirements for information skills
2.30pm to 3.00pm	Introduction of the Consultative Document
3.00pm to 3.15pm	Tea
3.15pm to 4.00pm	Three group discussions. The groups will comment on the document, discuss the present situation in schools and ask key questions: do we need to improve the situation? If so, how do we improve it?
4.00pm to 4.45pm	Plenary sessions. Groups report back and proposals for development for LEA, Governors, teaching staff and other relevant individuals and groups to be recorded.

Fig. 9.1

As a follow-up to the seminar for headteachers, the Schools Library Service sought to bring together those people involved in managing learning information resources on a day-to-day basis and organized seminars for heads of curriculum in schools together with the school's school librarian or teacher-librarian. The invitation sent out to schools made it clear that the seminar was being organized on the basis that *both* the school librarian and the senior teacher responsible for curriculum would attend. The advantages of such an approach are that the Schools Library Service is seen to concern itself with both the curriculum and resources (and not only library resources); the Service is seen to support both teachers and librarians; the senior teacher gains a clear appreciation of what the school librarian's role is in the school (and vice versa); the need for whole-school policies on resources (including information technology) provision is highlighted in a forum where interprofessional cooperation can be encouraged; and the status of the school librarian within her/his own school can be enhanced by attending a seminar on an equal basis with a member of the school's senior management.

Figure 9.2 outlines the seminar programme. The seminar was very successful and productive for both school librarians and teachers attending.

RESOURCE PROVISION: DEVELOPING A POLICY
A Schools Library INSET Workshop
for Senior Managers: Curriculum and School Librarians

Aims of the workshop
- To help schools analyse the implications for learning resources in new curriculum initiatives
- To enable schools to establish a policy for resource provision

Workshop outline

10am	Know your school
	Group work based on new plans and strategies
	Know your library
	What do you know and assume is going well?
	What is going badly?
11am	Who uses your library?
	Analysing your school library's relationship with the curriculum
	How do new initiatives affect this relationship?
12.30pm	Lunch
1.30pm-3pm	How can the library and the school come together?
	Group exercise
3pm	Tea
3.15pm	Plenary session
4.30pm	Close

Fig. 9.2

INSET – information skills and information technology
As stated above, Schools Library Services should not attempt to organize INSET seminars for either teachers or school librarians on the applications of information technology in isolation. There would be little point, for example, in organizing one-day courses for Cambridgeshire's school librarians on the use of CD-ROM or the selection of microcomputer software unless those attending were aware of the *context* in which CD-ROM or other software might be used. The key focus in Cambridgeshire's INSET programme has been the use of IT hardware and software with the development

of information skills in schools and the implications for learning, teaching and resources. The Schools Library Service organized a one-day seminar on the implications of the National Curriculum on the development of information skills in schools. The seminar was focused on science and the seminar was directed at heads of science/technology in schools and school librarians or teacher-librarians. As with the seminar on resource provision, attendance by one teacher and one librarian from each school was required.

Figure 9.3 outlines the seminar programme. As can be seen, the emphasis of the seminar was on the practicalities of developing information skills including examination of current schedules of work in schools.

NATIONAL CURRICULUM: DEVELOPING INFORMATION SKILLS
A Schools Library Service INSET Workshop

Aims of the course
- To identify in detail the information handling skills required by Science and Technology within the National Curriculum
- To identify ways in which these skills can be supported
- To explore the learning resource implications of developing information skills and achieving the ATs.

Course programme

9.30am	What information skills (including IT skills) are required by Science and Technology in the National Curriculum 1 – course participants to analyse a topic already set in KS3
10.15	What information skills (including IT skills) are required by Science and Technology 2 – more detailed analysis of all skills requirements of KS3, to be related to a 'standard' information skills framework
10.45	Coffee
11.15	Developing information skills – teaching/learning and resources implications
12.00	Planning for the teaching of information handling and use of learning resources (including IT resources) – group work on KS Science and Technology. Delegates are invited to bring along schemes of work
1.00	Lunch
2.00	The role of the library resource centre and of the librarian – group work
3.00	Tea
3.30	School and LEA support factors for the development of information-handling skills
4.30	Close

Fig. 9.3

Cambridgeshire LEA provides SIMS (School Information Management Systems) software to all its schools for a range of IT requirements. Cambridgeshire Schools Library Service has piloted the SIMS library module with the company and in cooperation with the information technology unit of the Education Department. INSET on SIMS has been done on a school-by-school basis, with Schools Library Service Staff visiting individual schools to train staff in the use of the SIMS library modules. A significant feature of the INSET in individual schools in relation to SIMS, is the emphasis on the information-retrieval elements in the package and this can be seen in Figure 9.4 which outlines the scope of a typical SIMS training day at a school.

The SIMS library module has been developed for use in schools to improve the management of resource centres in schools and to enhance the facilities for information retrieval within these resource centres.

The library module will be introduced in four parts, covering the different areas within the module, i.e.:

(a) Circulation
(b) Search
(c) Reports
(d) Management

Circulation
This covers the lending and return of resources to staff and pupils, as well as the facilities to reserve and renew resources.

Search
The Search facility is the most important aspect of SIMS as its use can be linked to the teaching of information-handling skills in the school. In Search mode, the system will allow the user to search the school's resources catalogue by:

Author
Title
Dewey number
Publisher
ISBN number
KEYWORDS

The ability of the user to search using keywords assigned to each resource is a significant improvement gained through using a computerized system. This has the advantages of facilitating greater use of the information contained in the resource centre's resources and giving staff and pupils greatly improved access to information scattered through the stock.

(cont.)

Reports

Statistics of the use of the resource centre's stock are compiled in the Reports section. This allows the librarian to analyse how individual pupils or groups of pupils have used the different areas of the resource centre.

Management

The catalogue records which form the basis of the library system are input in this part of the system as are other management parameters such as loan period and the number of resources per reader.

Hands-on practice with all elements of the system will be provided during the training day.

Fig. 9.4

To support the development of SIMS in school libraries in Cambridgeshire, the Schools Library Service has compiled a database entitled CAMBASE which covers the catalogue records held by schools in the county already using the SIMS library module. CAMBASE is a detailed keyworded subject index and is seen as an excellent aid in the teaching of information-retrieval skills in schools. As part of the INSET day in schools, school librarians are introduced to CAMBASE with a view to improving the keywording of resources. It is also stressed that the input of data, including keywords, in establishing a computerized library system is the most time-consuming element. It is also stressed to staff in the school (and not only in the school library) that this task is not a good use of professional library staff time and the use of CAMBASE can greatly cut the time needed to establish a computerized catalogue.

The use of information technology within Cambridgeshire schools' resource centres is put into the context of resource-based learning in INSET which takes the form of visits to particular schools by staff from other schools. Figure 9.5 shows an example of such a visit and it should be noted that included in the visit are discussions of resources policy, the role of the professional librarian and curricular aspects of resource-based learning. The importance of planning such visits in this way is to emphasize once again that the use of microcomputers in the school library has to be seen in the context of the curriculum and not in isolation. One problem this helps to avoid is the over-emphasis on the technical aspects of the library system or the use of CD-ROM and allows both teachers and school librarians to envisage the use of IT as another curricular resource.

CHESTERTON COMMUNITY COLLEGE
VISIT TO ST PETER'S SCHOOL, HUNTINGDON
Monday 6 April 1992

PROGRAMME

9.30	*Group 1* Tour of the resource centre The design and planning of a library resource centre A possible layout for Chesterton
	Group 2 The use of information technology within the centre SIMS library module CD-ROM
10.15	Coffee
10.30	*Group 1* The use of information technology within the centre SIMS library module CD-ROM
	Group 2 Tour of the resource centre The design and planning of a library resource centre A possible layout for Chesterton
11.15	A policy for learning resources The role of the professional librarian Resource-based learning across the curriculum
12.30	Close

Fig. 9.5

An extension of the INSET done by the Schools Library Service is the establishment of a SIMS Library Module User Group which is chaired by a member of the Schools Library Service and aims to explore further developments in and sophistication of SIMS, including networking. The group also discusses other developments in the use of computers in schools such as the use of CD-ROM and the availability of relevant software for use in schools.

One of the outcomes of INSET in relation to IT use has been the drawing up of bids by two Cambridgeshire schools in relation to the DES offer, 'Technology Schools Initiative', which sought bids from secondary schools for major IT developments. The schools have based their bids on their present library resource centres and the current developments which the Schools Library Service has supported including the use of the SIMS library module.

Evaluation

The importance of evaluating INSET in schools cannot be over-emphasized. Evaluation completes the training cycle and allows a new cycle to begin. The cycle begins with identifying the training needs of those involved in the management of learning resources in schools. This is followed by the establishment of a policy on INSET and what the strategy for INSET should be within the Schools Library Service. The planning and implementation of the strategy can then be carried out. The evaluation of INSET allows a fresh look at what new training needs have been identified since the start of the training cycle and also to what extent existing needs have been met. Evaluation is also important at a more detailed level and following each training session, wherever the session takes place, evaluation sheets are given to participants to allow feedback for the Schools Library Service but also to allow the participants in the INSET to evaluate the usefulness of the INSET session in relation to their own work in school. Figure 9.6 is an example of a training evaluation sheet used by the Education Service and the Schools Library Service in Cambridgeshire. It is important that evaluation sheets do not concentrate solely on the content of that day's INSET session. Important elements (as seen in Figure 9.6) include asking participants what they expected from the session before they came. Given that INSET is run for both teachers and school librarians from schools with different levels of resource provision and different experiences in the use of IT, it cannot be assumed that all participants will have the same expectations. Also, asking participants to state how they might follow up the INSET in their own school, serves two purposes. Firstly, it commits the teacher or the school librarian to thinking beyond the actual INSET day and, secondly, it allows the Schools Library Service to follow up at a later date the outcomes of the INSET, in relation to whether the participants *have* been able to follow up on the INSET day. Examples of how individual teachers or school librarians have followed up INSET days can also be used to motivate participants at subsequent INSET sessions.

CAMBRIDGESHIRE SCHOOLS LIBRARY SERVICE
INSET EVALUATION

Name . . . .
School . . . .
INSET attended . . . . National curriculum: developing information skills
Date . . . .
Venue . . . . Peterborough Educational Development Centre
Organiser . . . . Schools Library Service

(cont.)

1. Aims of this INSET
   To examine in detail the information handling skills required by Science and Technology within the National Curriculum
   To identify ways in which the development of these skills can be supported
   To explore the learning resource implications of developing information skills and achieving the ATs

2. What expectations did you have of this INSET?
[Participant's reply]
Suggestions of *practical* ways to improve information skills in the National Curriculum

3. Did this INSET add to your knowledge and experience?
[Participant's reply]
It was very useful in terms of reinforcing knowledge about information skills and the NC. An added bonus was being able to talk to other school librarians and to learn from their experiences and to exchange basic but very handy tips.

4. How will you your establishment follow up this INSET?
Short-term:
[Participant's reply]
Cascade what was learned here through departmental meetings in the school.
Long-term:
[Participant's reply]
Continue to work through HoDs to add information skills in schemes of work and, hopefully, by establishing a school policy on information skills work.

5. Please use this space to make any comments you wish about this INSET, including possible improvements. Please include comments about content, organization and tutors.
[Participant's reply]
Lots of food for thought – too much to digest immediately, but much to take back to school. The day was enjoyable and well organized and the speakers were very good. A good idea to have subjects attend as well, as this helped to fill gaps in our knowledge about both information skills and IT in the school.

Signature......................   Date......................

Fig. 9.6

Future developments

As Education Service central funds are increasingly delegated to schools, support services such as the Schools Library Service will become more accountable for why schools, especially secondary schools, want or need to buy back elements of the services provided. An area of increasing demand from the Schools Library Service is that of providing professional expertise on a loan basis, to support and advise schools on their own curricular developments, including the use of computers in all aspects of learning resource management, organization and use. As schools become more conscious of the need to become competitive, there is likely to be increased demand for INSET and professional advice in the areas of the development of library resource centres, the appointment of professional librarians and the extended use of computer software and hardware in the school library and in the school as a whole. Schools which can demonstrate that they have invested wisely and can provide the appropriate range of learning resources and their effective use by pupils and staff, are more likely to be seen by parents and governors to be providing an up-to-date, technologically relevant and educationally sound curriculum.

The developments in technology, particularly multimedia applications, will mean that the Schools Library Service will itself need constantly to update its staff on the potential use of IT in schools, as well as provide a constant flow of INSET sessions aimed at improving the skills of those involved in managing a school's information resources.

10 The future

James E. Herring

Reviewing the changes in educational policy, information technology applications and the increasingly complex roles of both teachers and school librarians over the past five years may appear to make any attempt to look at developments in the use of microcomputers in schools in the future an almost impossible task. It is useful, however, for all those involved in education to examine the *trends* in different areas of education in order that change can be anticipated, if not always totally prepared for. There are numerous short-term developments over the next five years which can be seen to be emerging already, e.g. the introduction of electronic mail systems in schools, but possibly longer-term forecasts such as online home/school links have to be treated with caution as these forecasts tend to be based on the opinions of individual authors rather than on detailed evidence from research. This chapter will examine future trends in the school curriculum, developments in hardware and software, school information systems, external sources of information, the role of the school librarian and the role of the school in an information society.

The school curriculum
Despite some changes of emphasis in schools with the introduction of the National Curriculum, the trend in schools towards a greater emphasis on pupils' learning abilities (as opposed to teachers' teaching abilities) is likely to continue and to be enhanced by the use of a variety of information technology applications in schools. Fothergill[1] argues that schools at the moment are in a transition period between the 'industrial curriculum' and a new curriculum for the post-industrial society. Fothergill argues that 'Today's curriculum is grounded within a clerical/verbal tradition where the nuances and record of words play an essential role in agreement and interpretation'[2] whereas the new curriculum is likely to utilize a much greater variety of resources. Fothergill further argues that the present curriculum is too inflexible, is still geared towards the

top 20 per cent of pupils and tends to be organized in a way in which pupils are taught in groups and at the same rate.

In some areas of today's curriculum in schools, it is clear that there is more emphasis on allowing pupils to work individually and at their own pace but this is often hidebound by a lack of suitable resources. If future pupils are to be allowed to learn effectively with materials which suit their own ability and their own learning style and if teachers are increasingly to become facilitators of learning in schools, there will need to be advances in the type of resources available to both pupils and teachers. The curricular resources of the future, in whatever format, will require to address not only *what* the pupil needs to know, but *how best* the pupil can acquire the knowledge and understanding related to the content of the resource. Thus a multimedia package on Democracy, available to a future pupil online in either the classroom or the school library, may be organized in such a way that it incorporates expert knowledge of the subject, allows interaction between the pupil and the package, stimulates the pupil to relate knowledge gained from the package to other areas of the curriculum and interprets the learning style and intellectual ability of the pupil in order that the individual pupil may gain an appropriate level and amount of knowledge from the package. This may seem a very idealistic picture but changes in technology are so rapid that the combination of existing interactive multimedia packages and the applications of expert systems may ensure that the arrival of 'smart' learning packages in schools will be sooner than expected.

One curricular trend that will continue is the emphasis on pupils learning to learn, including their ability to handle and use information effectively. Given that pupils are likely to have increasingly large amounts of information available to them, the ability of the individual pupil to select relevant information and, as importantly, to reject irrelevant information will be crucial. The fact that an individual pupil will be able to access information on Democracy from an online, full-text school library database as well as from external sources of information from local, national and international databases, certainly increases the *amount* of information available to pupils but the quality of learning for pupils will depend not on the quantity of information available to them but in the quality and relevance of the information, the appropriateness of the formats used, the level and style of language and images used, as well as the pupils' confidence and ability to select and use effectively the relevant information from that available. Thus a crucial question for tomorrow's curriculum for teachers and school librarians involved in organizing that curriculum, is whether pupils will be *dis*advantaged by having a plethora of resources available, in that it will be harder for them to select relevant ideas and information because they may feel threatened by the sheer quantity of information available.

Hardware and software

Forecasting developments in hardware and software in the short and medium term can be hazardous, given the variable rate of developments. For example, in the first edition of this book, CD-ROM applications were covered in the chapter on the future, whereas in this edition, there is a whole chapter dedicated to CD-ROM applications. One of the most important variables in certain applications achieving critical mass in education is government policy and the almost overnight conversion of schools to using CD-ROMs came partly as a result of a government-backed scheme to fund the purchase of CD-ROM equipment in all schools in the UK.

In the past five years, UK schools have moved on from using predominantly BBC microcomputers to more sophisticated hardware in the form of IBM-compatibles such as Nimbus, Amstrad and Acorn Archimedes as well as Apple Macintosh microcomputers. It is now not unusual for schools to have computer networks in computer laboratories in the school, and in the most advanced school libraries in the UK, networks are used *within* the library for a wide variety of applications. This trend toward greater sophistication in terms of memory size, quality of output (via laser printers) and ease of input (via scanners, optical character readers) in relation to microcomputer hardware will inevitably continue.

There have already been research projects[3] where pupils have been provided with portable computers to use in and out of school and, given the continuing decrease in the size of portable microcomputers and the continuing decrease in the cost of the hardware, it is not difficult to imagine a day when all pupils will, as standard, have a notebook microcomputer which can be linked to computerized networks in schools and which will contain software related to word-processing, spreadsheets, database and desktop publishing applications.

In terms of software, the emergence in five years of increasingly sophisticated hypertext[4] software has opened up new possibilities for teachers and school librarians to exploit. Hypertext programs such as Hypercard for the Apple Macintosh and Guide for PC compatibles allows the creation of sources of information which can be accessed in a way which reflects the information-seeking styles of individuals rather than the preferences of the compilers of the sources. Thus, in a traditional database system, the user searching for information is limited in searching to the use of keywords and Boolean logic (AND, OR, NOT) and it is difficult for the user to move from one area of the database to another. Hypertext systems are organized to allow greater choice for the individual user to look for the information which s/he seeks at any particular point. Words, phrases or even pictures can be programmed as 'buttons' and, when a button is highlighted, more information on the word, phrase or picture can be given immediately. Thus a pupil searching a hypertext database on Mozart could have the choice of finding out about Mozart's works, his family or his environment by highlighting one of these aspects as opposed to creating new search strategies as with a traditional database. One current example of hypertext use is in Lynn Grove High School in Great Yarmouth where pupils, using Hypercard on an Apple Macintosh network, created a hypertext database of a bridge disaster in Great Yarmouth in 1845, as part of a history project. The pupils used burial records, census information and contemporary newspaper articles to build a series of 'stacks' of information on different aspects of the disaster. Pupils also scanned in 19th-century maps of the region so that the geographical location of those killed in the disaster could be shown. The result, according to a teacher involved with the project, was that the pupils had used Hypercard to 'provide a sophisticated, yet simple to use information retrieval system that allows access to computer based curriculum material produced by staff and pupils'.[5]

Future developments in hypertext systems lie in the creation of multimedia sources on CD-ROM-type disks. Both commercially produced sources and in-house materials are likely to be available. In the future, teachers and pupils will be able to save large amounts of information, in the form of text, graphics, photographs, video and sound on disks which can be written to (unlike CD-ROM disks) and fifth- and sixth-generation programming languages will enable the creation of sophisticated packages, geared to the needs of individual schools or individual groups of pupils, without the need for expert programming knowledge. Hypertext is probably the most exciting new software development in education today.

Other developments in software will relate to the increasing sophistication of expert systems. As with hypertext, the development of fifth- and sixth-generation programming languages will more easily allow the creation of learning packages which encompass the knowledge of the expert, e.g. the teacher, in a school. If expert systems on particular curricular topics can be developed at both national and local levels, this may free teachers from much of the introductory work they do in introducing concepts to pupils. An expert system on aspects of Urban geography, for example, could explain to pupils what urban geography is, what areas of study are contained within the topic, what resources are available to pupils and could incorporate interactive sections where pupils would be 'taught' by the computer and then assessed on their knowledge at different stages and given feedback on their responses.

At present, expert systems even on very narrow topics are time-consuming to create and still relatively simple. Systems are created by 'knowledge engineers' who incorporate the knowledge of an expert, e.g. a doctor, into a package. In the future, the time taken and expertise needed to create expert systems is likely to decrease dramatically and, for school librarians and teachers, the creation of 'expert' databases holding information contained in the school library and in classrooms is an exciting prospect. No such expert systems exist as yet but it may be that some of the problems of information retrieval faced by pupils who require to search huge amounts of information, as seen above, may be solved by sophisticated expert databases. It may be, for example, that instead of the pupil searching the expert database, the database will 'search' the pupil's mind in order to identify the exact nature of the pupil's enquiry. In this way, we may see an extension of the role of the microcomputer in enhancing the information skills of pupils in the future.

A further development in software in the future is likely to lie in voice-activated systems. Such systems do exist at present but are not used in schools. Voicemed, for example, is a voice-activated system which helps doctors to produce patient reports. The computer produces a word-processed version of the doctor's speech on screen and this can be used as a computerized record or as the basis of a letter to a hospital or to the patient. In schools, voice-activated databases in the school library would allow pupils to interrogate the database by verbally asking questions as opposed to typing in enquiries. The advantages of this may be limited as voice activation in itself will not improve the quality of the pupil's search strategy and the advantage may be purely technical. For pupils with a handicap, voice-activated systems could provide them with previously denied access to a wide variety of information sources. However, the information skills of such pupils will still need to be sophisticated enough to allow them to search bibliographic and full-text sources effectively.

School information systems

As with CD-ROM, there has been a rapid development in schools towards fully integrated school information systems since the first edition of this book. Networks of various levels of sophistication now exist in many schools and access to centrally held software packages is now available from different parts of the school. At this stage, schools are still developing information systems and the introduction of fully integrated systems is still hindered mainly by cost but it is likely that in the next five to ten years most schools will develop LANs (local area networks) similar to those which already exist in universities and colleges across the country.

The advantages for all school staff and for pupils are potentially enormous. The linking of the school library system to every classroom (which would have at least one terminal) as well as to existing networks in computer laboratories or IT workshops would allow instant information retrieval for pupils and teachers. For example, a history teacher examining the civil rights movement in the USA could, instead of asking pupils (as at present) to check the speeches of Martin Luther King in the library at a later date, allow pupils to go directly online to the school library system and retrieve a speech in sound and video which the whole class or an individual pupil or a group of pupils could watch. This would be a dramatic advance in the use of information in schools at the point of need. One of the great drawbacks faced by teachers wishing to encourage pupils to make greater use of library resources and by school librarians attempting to create more access for pupils to the school library, has been that, at present, in order to retrieve information of any kind, the pupil must go to the library. In future, the library may come to the pupil or to the teacher anywhere in the school.

In the TV series *Doctor Who*, the Doctor has a superlative information system called a Tardis. One of the features of a Tardis is that from the outside it looks very small but once inside, the Doctor has a huge variety of computers and space in which to use them. A future school library or school information centre may have similar features to a Tardis. It may well be physically smaller, in that more and more sources of information, at present in print form, will be in electronic format but the school library, in information terms, will be several times larger than existing libraries because of the amount of information held in its information systems. Pupils accessing the system will be able to download text, sound and video and, in the longer term, holographs and virtual-reality packages to stimulate learning experiences.

In the short term, the design and development of school information systems should be based on a planning process in which both teachers and school librarians should be involved. School librarians in particular should ensure that the school library is not overlooked in the planning of new systems. Indeed, it may be that in the future, school information managers (see below) will be appointed to oversee the school's total information and information technology needs.

One emerging feature of school information systems which is likely to be widespread in a few years is the use of electronic mail (e-mail). In a few schools in the UK, projects have been established to introduce and to evaluate electronic mail systems in secondary schools. E-mail systems are based on each user (pupil, teacher, librarian, administrator) having a user name and a password. The user name will be in the form of, for example, 1P1THOM , who could be a pupil from class 1P1 with a surname Thomson. The password will be a word or a sequence of letters known only to the user and changed at intervals for security purposes. On accessing the system, the user will input his/her user name which will appear on the screen and then his/her password which will *not* appear on the screen, so that other users cannot have access to personal mail. Once in the system, the user will be offered choices of reading mail sent to him/her or of sending mail to an individual or group. 'Mail' can be in the form of a simple message, e.g. examination timetable or time and place of a meeting, or a more substantial document, perhaps the outline of a lesson (sent from teacher to all pupils in a class) or a draft essay (sent from pupil to teacher). There are almost endless possibilities in the use of e-mail in schools, especially if use is made of bulletin boards or teleconferencing facilities.

The NECT report *Online: E-mail in the curriculum*, based on an e-mail research project, states that e-mail systems should only be established in schools where there is a clear curricular purpose for such a system: 'There is little point in using electronic communications just for the sake of it, even if it does fulfil some of the requirements of the National Curriculum. As a sterile exercise in a technology class, it is likely to be quickly forgotten.' The report argues that potential uses of e-mail in the curriculum could be in areas where

> pupils need or could benefit from
> - text from others which can be manipulated in some way – put into another format or edited perhaps
> - fast responses to questions or pieces of writing
> - the views of others
> - communication with others abroad
> - contact with many others at the same time
> - contact with an unknown audience
> - an element of fantasy, role play or simulation
> - discussion with others from different backgrounds

- 'invisible' links where value judgements cannot be made about their partners based on appearance, sex, race, age or handwriting
- first hand information – factual or impressionistic – from other pupils[6]

One example of e-mail contacts with European schools is a project based in Redhill School in Stourbridge, where pupils used the Interspan system to link up with schools in Europe and receive articles for a European schools newspaper.[7]

Electronic mail will be one of a number of features in a future school information system and it will be those schools in which teachers and school librarians identify the information *needs* of pupils, teachers, school librarians and others in school and then develop appropriate systems to meet these needs, which will benefit most from school information systems. Schools which install off-the-shelf systems first and then examine how they might use the systems may well find that they will regret their lack of planning.

External sources of information

As can be seen from chapters 5 and 6, schools already have some access to external sources of information via online systems. This is another area where, depending on costs, rapid developments could take place. For example, following the trend set in academic libraries, school librarians in the future may have access to the catalogues of other school libraries in their areas or to the catalogues of academic libraries nation-wide. On the face of it, this may not seem to be a great advantage to pupils, teachers and school librarians. The fact that a pupil can establish the *existence* of a source of information does not help that pupil to *use* that source for a project unless it can quickly be obtained through interlibrary loan. Similarly, teachers using systems such as NERIS may also be frustrated by the time it takes to order materials.

One possible solution to this problem is electronic publishing and the electronic library. An electronic library may be envisioned as one where *all* materials – print, audiovisual, video, computer-based – are available in electronic format and may be sent down a line to a remote user. In an ideal world, pupils in all schools would have access to all learning materials held in electronic libraries. There are, however, many practical difficulties in this scenario. Copyright is a major stumbling block. If a teacher or pupil in a school downloads parts (or all) of a newly published book on Space travel, will s/he have to pay for this access? If not, how will publishers profit from publishing the book? If so, how will schools afford to access such resources? There are many implications for the quality of resources available to schools in relation to electronic publishing but once effective systems of charging are worked out, the access to information outside the school could be revolutionized.

For school librarians, there are many implications especially with regard to incorporating downloaded material into the school's existing databases. The ability of pupils and teachers to retrieve information downloaded from external sources and to reuse that information for a different curricular purpose from that of the original one, will depend on the effectiveness of the retrieval system in the school's information system. As noted above, school librarians and teachers will be aware that the need for pupils to be able to cope with large amounts of information will be even more important when external sources can be easily accessed.

The role of the school librarian and the teacher
Changes in technology affect the roles of professionals in all walks of life and schools are no different. Teachers and school librarians face a future in which change will be constant. Both will be expected to evaluate continually new technological innovations either in the format of learning resources or in the delivery systems required to access such resources. This evaluation will relate to the quality of learning resources and their suitability for the school's curriculum. Inservice training in evaluating and using new forms of learning resources will be vital for both professions because of the in-built obsolescence of resources caused by constant technological improvement. It is not inconceivable that eventually the two professions will merge, with school librarians taking on more of a teaching role and teachers increasingly becoming facilitators in providing access to relevant information sources and in teaching learning skills. Teachers will be much more technologically aware than they are today and each school may employ one or two teachers whose role is to create learning packages using advanced programming languages.

For school librarians, the immediate future will see their role as being increasingly linked to technological developments in the school library and within the school as a whole. As the education for school librarians broadens into the wider domain of information management, school librarians may adopt new titles such as school information manager or learning resources manager and this will reflect their role as coordinators of information on a school-wide basis and not merely within the school library. Some school librarians in the future may include knowledge engineering and the creation of expert systems in their role. The role of the school librarian as expert on new hardware and software and on external sources of information is likely to expand if school librarians are encouraged via professional training and extensive INSET to widen their role. If this does not happen, school librarians could find themselves locked in an increasingly outdated role as managers of print-based collections whilst others are responsible for electronic learning resources. The role of school library services managers is vital in this area, as they are the professionals who perhaps will have most influence on how school librarians' skills are utilized in schools.

The future for school librarians as educational information professionals is an exciting one, in that, given the skills, the drive and the energy required, they may be key professionals in providing pupils with quality education in schools and with the necessary information skills required in an information society.

The school in an information society

There has been much speculation about the future of the school itself. Will Stonier and Conlin's[8] view that for pupils 'home will become the place to go to learn − school, where you play' be true in the information society discussed by writers such as Martin?[9] The protagonists of home-based learning tend to be very optimistic about the access to both equipment and information services by everyone in society. Their view is that all homes will be linked to schools and that advanced learning packages will allow pupils to learn more effectively in the home environment. Other commentators are less optimistic, seeing possible dangers in the cost to individual families of home − school technological links and the possibility of a divided society in which quality education is only available to those who can afford it. Cawkell puts it succinctly: 'There is the spectre of information deprivation amongst information abundance'.[10]

There is genuine fear that in an information society education will be more important than ever and that pupils who attend or are linked to technologically advanced schools will have the advantage in terms of entering higher education and gaining the well-paid information-related jobs available whilst their counterparts in poorer schools will have less access to advanced information technology and less prospect of entering the information professions of the future. Whether this fear is realized or not will depend on social, economic and political decisions taken, particularly by future governments. The availability of information technology greatly more sophisticated than at present does not determine its creative use. The influences of class and wealth on future education will have to be different from their influence on present-day education if genuine equality of educational opportunity is to be realized in the future. The technology will provide the means for greatly increased access for all to educational resources which may be able to take on some of the roles at present played by teachers and school librarians, but the distribution of this technology and the *actual* access gained by pupils from schools in different socio-economic areas will depend on funding to a great extent.

Whether future pupils are educated at school or partly at home, Fothergill argues that 'Crucial to the information society is the ability to handle and use information'[11] and this will be true wherever learning takes place and whatever level of technology is used. The term 'information society' implies that all the key aspects of that society, including education and employment, will relate to information, its creation, retrieval and use. Teachers and school librarians, as educational professionals whose main focus is the encouragement of learning, should have key roles in an information society which, it is hoped, will widen access to learning and learning resources throughout the world.

References

1 Fothergill, R., *Implications of new technology for the school curriculum*, Kogan Page, 1988.
2 ibid., 116.
3 *Times educational supplement*, 7 June 1991, 46.
4 See, for example: McAleese, R., *Hypertext: the state of the art*, Intellect Ltd, 1990.
5 *Times educational supplement update: computers*, Nov. 1991, 9.
6 NCET, *Online: e-mail in the curriculum*, NCET, 1991.
7 *Times educational supplement*, 7 June 1991, 44.
8 Stonier, T. and Conlin, C., *The three Cs*, Wiley, 1985.
9 Martin, W., *The information society*, Aslib, 1988.
10 Cawkell, A. E., 'The real information society', *Journal of information science*, **12** (3), 1986.
11 Fothergill, R., op.cit., 174.

Appendix 1 Software and supplier's list
(See Chapter 8)

1 North Polar Expedition (Virgin Interactive) 081-960 2255.
2 PC Globe (Djanogly CTC) 0602 424422.
3 Census 1981 (Chadwick Healey) 0223 311479.
4 Windows Workstation (Roderick Manhattan) 071-978 1727.
5 Big Black Catalogue (AVP) 0291 625439.
6 Software catalogue (Action Computer Supplies) 0800 333333.
7 Basic Skills Software Guide (ALBSU) 071-405 4017.
8 Careers Software Review (NCET) 0203 416994.
9 Educational Software (Whitaker/NCET) 071-836 8911.
10 The CD-ROM directory (TFPL) 071-251 5522.
11 PC Yearbook (VNU Business Publications) 071-439 4242.
12 CHEST Software Directory (Bath University Press) 0225 826036.
13 NERIS 0525 290364.
14 Encyclopedia of Mammalian Biology (McGraw-Hill) 0628 23432.
15 Science and Technical Reference Set (McGraw-Hill) 0628 23432.
16 Word for Windows 2.0 0734 270000 for list of dealers.
17 Pagemaker (Aldus) 031-220 4747.
18 Ecodisc (MultiMedia Corporation) 071-722 7595.
19 RISC-OS CD-ROMs 0483 503121.
20 Healthdata – 21 Vicars Close, London E9 7HT.
21 Tick Tack (Primrose Publishing) 0284 811185.
22 Soutron Library System 0602 441644.

Appendix 2   SIMS library module

SIMS

MAIN FEATURES OF THE SYSTEM

Library Management System

System Overview

> The SIMS Library Management System will run on most 16 and 32 bit
> business computers under MS-DOS, either on a network, or on a stand-
> alone machine with at least 40Mb hard disk storage. It is designed for
> network use, so that, for example, one station can be used in the Librarian's
> office, one or two on the issues desk, and several around the library for
> student use. In addition, the system can be accessed by any other
> computer in the school which is on the same network, bringing the school's
> resources within easy reach of the whole school community. It can be used
> to manage effectively a wide range of school resources, including books,
> videos, periodicals, computer software and other resources

The aim has been twofold:–
One; to provide a tool for use by Librarians and Resource Centre Managers
for organising, managing, and recording the movement of the resources
for which they have responsibility

Two; a means of providing a service to their users, enabling direct access to
information about the resources available to them

Cataloguing

> The system allows the construction of a catalogue of all available resources,
> with recording of individual information, and keywording on each item.
> Information is collected and cross referenced by the system as it is entered,
> in order to facilitate search and reporting routines for retrieval of
> information, in a useful way, when required. Lists of collected information
> are available to the user on screen at all stages of the process, from entry
> to retrieval, by the use of the F1 help key and the chosen selection key

Cataloguing Facilities

> SIMS Library system provides up to 100 characters for a title, up to three
> authors, publisher automatically sensed from ISBN, owner/location, dewey
> code, date published, date purchased, cost, up to 20 keywords, flags for
> reference or fiction, user-defined resource types, and traps. Multiple copies
> are catered for, and entry and editing is done by full-screen editing with
> context-sensitive field selection facilities to reduce keystrokes and ensure
> consistency. Catalogue data may be imported: for example, from Whitaker's
> Bookbank on CD ROM (SIMS interface is available). File size is limited only
> by the size of the hard disc

Borrower Records

> Borrower records can be constructed individually or through the interface
> with STAR and will be added to by the system as the circulation system is
> accessed

Appendix 3   3M security system

What price would you put on book losses in your library?

If you haven't installed a 3M book detection system you may say hundreds, or possibly thousands, of pounds.

But however considerable the financial implications may be, there are other ways in which you can lose too.

There's the time lost looking for books that can affect the function and management of a library. There's the lost credibility with patrons in not fulfilling their requests and a consequential loss of morale amongst library staff.

Library prestige too can be lost if important or irreplaceable books cannot be made readily available or accessible.

Furthermore, why dilute your budget allocation by replacing stolen books when you could be investing in new material?

The 3M Connection

With over 1000 book detection systems installed in libraries of all types throughout the United Kingdom, we can justifiably call ourselves the most experienced company in library security today.

Our comprehensive range of equipment has been designed to meet the varying requirements of the many different types and sizes of library to be found in the public, educational and specialist sectors.

And our service and after-sales back-up is everything that you would expect from such a reliable and established company.

How the System works

We're not prepared to show or describe in this brochure exactly what is at the heart of the system. That would put the integrity of the product at risk.

However, in very simple, broad terms there are two basic elements. One is a device or 'trigger' that is fitted very easily into each book – hardback, paperback or magazine. This trigger is very discreet and when

Library with an 1850 single corridor system.

concealed within the book is virtually undetectable.

The other is a free-standing sensing unit at the exit of the library.

Books left on the shelf are sensitised and remain so until a book to be borrowed by a patron is desensitised at the issue desk by library staff, and the patron then exits normally.

If, however, a patron attempts to steal or forgetfully walks out with a book that has not been desensitised, the trigger sets off an alarm within the sensing unit and the exit gate locks.

Triggered books are sensitised/desensitised by library staff using a small book check unit.

Books cannot be shielded by the human body, bags or conventional briefcases. The system cannot affect the health of patrons either; it does not emit X-ray, radio or microwaves.

Which system will suit your library?

The size and type of library you have will probably determine what sort of 3M system you want to install and how to manage it.

There are two sizes of system available, although both can be supplemented or modified to suit your circumstances from a range of ancillary equipment.

For libraries with a high volume of traffic, the model 1850 system is recommended. This can be supplied in either single or dual exit corridor versions, depending on your entrance/exit requirements.

The model 1365 system is particularly good for smaller libraries or where budgets are particularly restrictive.

Both the model 1850 and model 1365 book detection systems can work in Full Circulating or By-Pass modes.

Academic library with a 1365 system.

Bibliography

Akers, N., *Freefax*, SLG, 1989.

Allen, J. P., 'Information technology across the curriculum', *Computer education*, June 1991.

Birnbaum, I., *The place of information technology in the secondary curriculum*, MUSE, 1986.

Carter, C. and Monaco, J., *Learning information technology skills*, British Library, 1987.

Cawkell, A. E., 'The real information society', *Journal of information science*, **12** (3), 1986.

CD-ROM resources list, NCET, 1991.

CD-ROMs in print 1992, Meckler, 1992.

Condon, J., *Letting the information world into your school: the use of the modem*, SLG, 1987.

Condon, J., 'Present users into future users', in *Online information 88*, Learned Information, 1988.

Conlon, T. and Cope, P. (eds.), *Computing in Scottish education : the first decade and beyond*, Edinburgh University Press, 1989.

Department of Education and Science, *Information technology from 5 to 16*, HMSO, 1989.

Department of Education and Science, *Technology in the National Curriculum*, HMSO, 1990.

Donnelly, J. (ed.), *The school management handbook*, Kogan Page, 1992.

Evans, N., *The future of the microcomputer in schools*, Macmillan Education, 1986.

Fothergill, R., *Implications of new technology for the school curriculum*, Kogan Page, 1988.

Griffin, J. A. and Davies, S., 'IT in the National Curriculum', *Journal of computer assisted learning*, **6**, 1990.

Hall, J. L., *Online bibliographic databases: a directory and sourcebook*, Aslib, 1986.

Herring, J. E. (ed.), *The microcomputer, the school librarian and the teacher*, Bingley, 1987.

Information skills and the National Curriculum, NCET, 1990.

Irving, A. *Wider horizons: online information services in schools*, British Library, 1990.

McAlese, R., *Hypertext: the state of the art*, Intellect Ltd, 1990.

McDonald, S., 'IT in the National Curriculum: the view from Scotland', *Journal of computer assisted learning*, 7, 1991.

Mapp, L., 'Knowledge at your fingertips', *Teacher's weekly*, 7 March 1991.

Markless, S. and Lincoln, P., *Tools for learning: information skills and learning to learn in secondary schools*, British Library, 1986.

Marland, M. (ed.), *Information skills in the secondary curriculum*, Methuen Educational, 1981.

Martin, W., *The information society*, Aslib, 1988.

Matthews, S., *CD-ROMs in school libraries*, British Library, 1990.

National Curriculum Council, *Technology in the National Curriculum: non statutory guidance: information technology capability*, HMSO, 1990.

Learning geography with computers pack, NCET, 1990.

Online: email in the curriculum, NCET, 1991.

Online information services for schools: a select list, NCET, 1990.

Preston, C., 'Reading the news', *Educational computing and technology*, **13** (2), Feb. 1992.

Royce, C. *et al.*, *CD-ROM: usage and prospects*, British Library, 1989.

Sansom, S., *Campus 2000 user guide*, British Telecom, 1991.

Somekh, B. and Davies, R., 'Towards a pedagogy for information technology', *The curriculum journal*, **2** (2), Summer 1991.

Stonier, T. and Conlin, C., *The three Cs*, Wiley, 1985.

Times educational supplement, 8 Mar. 1991.

Times educational supplement, update: Computers, Nov. 1991.

Williams, D. and Herring, J. E., *Keywords and learning*, RGIT, 1986.

Index